Collins
MUSIC

How to teach
Instrumental
& singing
lessons

100
INSPIRING IDEAS

Karen Marshall and Penny Stirling

MIX
Paper from
responsible sources
FSC C007454

This book is produced from independently certified FSC paper
to ensure responsible forest management.

For more information visit: **www.harpercollins.co.uk/green**

William Collins' dream of knowledge for all began with the publication of his first book in 1819.
A self-educated mill worker, he not only enriched millions of lives, but also founded a flourishing publishing house. Today, staying true to this spirit, Collins books are packed with inspiration, innovation and practical expertise. They place you at the centre of a world of possibility and give you exactly what you need to explore it. Collins. Freedom to teach.

An imprint of HarperCollins*Publishers*
The News Building
1 London Bridge Street
London
SE1 9GF

www.collins.co.uk

Text © Karen Marshall 2017
Text © Penny Stirling 2017
Design © HarperCollins*Publishers* 2017

10 9 8 7 6 5 4 3 2 1

ISBN 978-1-4729-2739-2

British Library Cataloguing in Publication Data A catalogue record for this publication is available from the British Library.

Commissioning editor: Mary Chandler
Development editor: Em Wilson
Project editor: Alexander Rutherford
Proofreader: Sue Chapple
Cover designer: Angela English
Internal designer: Ken Vail Graphic Design
Production controller: Sarah Burke
Printed and bound by Caligraving Ltd

Acknowledgements

From Karen: Many thanks to Adam, my tolerant and patient husband, and my three children – Jacob, Anna and Naomi – your loving support makes all my writing possible. Many thanks to my writing partner, Heather Hammond, for her ongoing checking over of the script and to Rowan Cozens for allowing me to include her anecdote (Idea 26). I dedicate this book to my Uncle and Auntie, the late Derek Oldman (2015) and Rosemary Beresford (2016) who both worked hard in their communities helping people and in turn making lives better.

From Penny: Huge thanks to Graham Merriam, my long-suffering husband and lover of music, who is an incredibly helpful mobile encyclopedia. I dedicate this book to my many students who have put up with my questioning and sometimes over-enthusiastic approach and still managed to go on, some to extraordinarily successful lives as musicians, others just to love and enjoy music.

Finally, we would like to thank the special Mary Chandler (Collins Music Publishing Manager) – a real talent in music publishing who is a joy to work with!

Table of contents

Progression

Beyond lessons

Business bits and practicalities

Introduction

As a practising instrumental and singing teacher, you have to be a jack of all trades! From accountant to child psychologist, teaching one-to-one and in groups and yes, since wider opportunities, 30 children together in a classroom – all these skills may need to be called on. You have to be able expertly to teach music theory as well as train someone's aural skills to identify chord sequences and not to crack when having to sight-sing (even if singing is not their thing!).

Luckily in our own careers we've had lots of brilliant music teachers around us who have shared their talents and given us hints and tips on the way. With over 60 years experience between us, we've successfully taught lots of lessons (and sometimes not – we have at times learnt the hard way!). Our students have also taught us much! We sincerely hope that *How to Teach: Instrumental and singing lessons* will make your working life just that little bit easier; that it will provide a pocketful of ideas that will help your students achieve their musical potential, and that when you feel like you've tried everything to help them learn all those scales or master their performance anxiety, an idea within these pages will help shed new light on the situation.

These are just ideas. You as the teacher really are the expert on how best to use them within your teaching, but at every turn we would ask you to consider our two fundamental ideas:

◉ **Is my teaching MUSIC-focused?** Is music at the centre of my teaching, so that at every possible turn I am teaching music through music and developing a joy of it in my student?

◉ **Is my teaching STUDENT-focused?** Am I teaching based on the individual needs of each of my students? Is it helping my students achieve their musical potential whilst also meeting their personal needs and ambitions around music? Is my teaching all about my student and not all about me?

We all have the privilege of working with students at a very formative time in their lives; you can make a real difference to their confidence, resilience, adaptability and ability to work on their own (skills they can use throughout their lives). Do look after yourself too!

Good luck!

Penny and Karen

How to use this book

Dip into this book whenever you want a flash of inspiration to improve and inspire your instrumental/singing teaching.

The ideas in this book are organised by theme – these are given at the foot of each page. Each idea follows a very simple format:

○ **Title:** the catchy title sums up what the idea is about.

○ **Quote:** the opening quote from a teacher or student captures the essence of the idea.

○ **Overview:** the quick overview of the idea will help you select a new idea to read or re-find an idea you found useful on a previous flick-through.

○ **Idea:** the idea itself.

○ **Hints and tips:** additional teaching tips, suggestions for ways to take the idea further, anecdotes and bonus ideas are provided throughout.

Communication **1**

"My teacher really cares about me and always makes me feel as if I'm the most important person!"

Communication is a two-way process that can affect a student's whole development. It is not just about exchanging information, but sometimes reading the emotion behind the information in order to fully understand the meaning of what is being said.

Be reliable

❍ Have a standard form for all students/parents to complete which includes *all* contact details: home phone, work phone (for emergencies only), mobile number, email addresses, home address.

❍ Use a simple 'old-fashioned' filing system so you have a back-up when you lose your mobile phone!

Involve parents and carers

❍ Face-to-face contact is easier and regular contact ensures nobody feels 'left out'. Invite parents to pop in for the last five minutes of lessons so that you can keep them in touch with progress – or ask for some practice support if needed.

Always strive to inspire

❍ Don't just send out factual information – we all stop reading those emails! – email parents/students about exciting events/concerts too, especially if you can negotiate cheap tickets.

❍ Always try to have time to listen. Although it can sometimes be difficult, dealing with a situation immediately can prevent things festering. 'Nip it in the bud' is very sound advice.

Stay professional

❍ With the current ability to transmit information instantly online, ensure all communications are strictly professional. Scream at the wall if you need to, but don't put it in print!

Keep in touch

❍ Arrange to see old students whenever you can. They always appreciate a cup of tea and a chat and it keeps the lines of progression open for the future.

> **Top tip**
>
> The importance of being a good listener is paramount: make whoever you are talking to feel valued and listened to by giving good eye contact and having a relaxed body posture.

2 Teaching about performance

"The most helpful thing any performer can be given is confidence in their ability to succeed."

Teaching an instrument is not just about the basic necessity of learning the notes, it is about teaching someone to be a musician. Help your students become performers from the start and make learning to perform part of your teaching.

Here are some ideas to get you started:

❍ Start early: Build up a positive attitude to performance from the very first eight-bar piece so that your students see it as a regular thing that they do. Encourage playing in front of an 'audience' (from just other students up to larger groups) to instil a sense of performing.

❍ Check that the instrument is in good condition: Worrying about a string that might break or a dodgy reed immediately before a performance is an unnecessary extra in the worry list.

❍ Make accuracy a given: If the preparation and practice has been good, then confidence and accuracy should be high. A good performance comes when your students are able to leave thoughts about accuracy behind and concentrate on 'painting a picture' for the audience.

> ### Anecdote 🗨
>
> I once accompanied a young cellist in their final lesson before an important performance. The playing was pretty grim so I was staggered to hear the teacher say that she was sure it would be a wonderful concert. Later she told me, 'The night before a concert I can't change anything so I try to give a confidence boost'.

❍ Memory is good: Playing from memory is, for some, something that you just 'do'. However, it does need to be taught. Work to build up the 'memory bank' for all your students from the very early lessons.

❍ Build an understanding of 'what ifs': 'The shakes' can be caused simply by a burst of adrenalin when excitement kicks in. Understanding that this is a short burst and will quickly dissipate if allowed to flow away, can help.

❍ Compliments are good: After the performance, ensure comments are always positive (the place for reflection on the performance is in the next lesson, *not* the foyer). Particularly beware of the overly critical parent who can all too easily destroy your good work.

Mrs Curwen's maxims 3

"Mrs Curwen's maxims are so insightful!"

Mrs Curwen was a teacher writing materials for piano and music teachers at the turn of the 20th century. Her ethos can be seen in some of the most respected music education approaches such as Kodály. Her 12 educational maxims include teaching concepts on how to manage content and progression. Here are four.

Maxim 1: 'Teach the easy before the difficult'

Students gain far more confidence if there is something they can do easily. This confidence then helps them to achieve the more difficult tasks.

Maxim 2: 'Teach the thing before the sign'

An easier way to understand the value of this is through the other common expression, 'sound before symbol'. A child can more easily play forte if they hear what good forte playing is. After this, the forte sign can be introduced and understood.

Maxim 7: 'Proceed from the known to the related unknown'

Children work well if they can make connections. Just as you need to know the alphabet before you can start reading words, it helps to understand what 3/8 time is before you learn about 6/8. A student will then already understand that 8 represents a quaver.

Maxim 11: 'Never tell a child anything that you can help them discover for themselves'

If a child plays a passage with incorrect notes or rhythm, simply play their version, followed by the correct version and invite them to spot the difference.

Top tip

If a student is particularly struggling with a concept, start with the known and develop from there. Continue by breaking the elements of learning into much smaller steps.

Taking it further...

Mrs Curwen's maxims are from *Mrs Curwen's Pianoforte Method: The Teacher's Guide* (London 1913).

Bonus idea

Students often simply say they understand something when sometimes they haven't got a clue. Play the game: 'Can you teach me to do that?' It soon becomes very clear whether the student understands what you've taught, and sometimes they will show you better ways to teach them!

4 Willingness to learn and grow

"A good teacher is a willing learner."

As teachers, we can develop particular ways of working and favourite materials to use. It is important to remember that things move on and change with new technology, more books published and a greater range materials.

Are you humble as a teacher or do you always think your way is right or best? Or, have you not really thought about it? It is important to remember that teaching isn't black and white. Your preferred way of working wouldn't be wrong, but there might be some new fresh approach that can better meet the needs of a particular student.

Here are our top tips for developing a willingness to learn and grow as a teacher:

● **Be open to new ideas** – don't make the assumption that something won't work unless you've tried it out (more than once).

● **Try to experiment regularly with new ways of working** – try a different way to teach a scale or the words to a song, or explore new ways to motivate and incentivise your students.

● **Remember the saying 'a change is as good as a rest'** – you may be re-invigorated by using a new tutor book and introducing a composer you've never taught before.

● **Check out all the Facebook groups or forums** – you might find solutions to any teaching difficulties there if you look!

● **Access master classes** – contact your local music hub or even university music department.

Top tip

Ask a colleague if they will allow you to observe their teaching. How do they work differently from you? What can you take from their work and implement into your teaching? Alternatively, video your own teaching and review it. You may be surprised at what you notice.

Bonus idea

Visit a large music shop or exhibition (e.g. Rhinegold's Music Education EXPO) and review all the latest materials and publications.

Teacher–student relationship 5

"My religion is kindness." Dalai Lama

Kindness can go a long way with our students, especially when other things in their life can be difficult – their home life, coping with family illnesses or bereavements, struggling with friendships or school examinations...

Being a kind teacher can take several forms:

○ **Value your students' feelings:** Try to value your students' thoughts when they talk to you about what they feel. Reflect back to them if they are finding something difficult. For example, if they say to you: 'I just can't remember my scales!', instead of simply acknowledging that scales are not easy, consider how you might be able to help, e.g. 'Perhaps the way we have tried is not the easiest for you, so let's find another way that works better for you.'

○ **Be interested:** Be interested in what your student has to tell you; be willing to hear and listen to their stories, even if they are not relevant to the lesson – it helps your student to feel valued by you.

○ **Give praise:** When the opportunity arises, be generous with your praise and find every opportunity to do so. However, there is a balance here. Remember, children and adults are very good at self-evaluation. Your praise will become less valuable if you praise when it is not really deserved.

○ **Think kindness:** Make it a regular habit to think, how can I deal with this situation in the most kindly way. Have as your aim that if your student was asked: 'Is your teacher kind?' they would without hesitation say 'Yes!'.

Top tip

Provide a welcoming teaching environment (starting with a smile). Ensure your students know that your time and concentration is focused entirely on them with no phone calls, emails or text messages.

Anecdote

A student once told me that their friend hadn't turned up to their lesson because they had forgotten their music. The next week I told all my students that I would never be cross if they forgot their music and had a supply of music just in case (spare copies, duets, sight reading and easy fun repertoire). Missed lessons have reduced significantly ever since!

6 What makes a good instrumental/singing teacher?

"There is more to this job than meets the eye...!"

There are many traits to a good instrumental/singing teacher. This idea gives a snapshot of some of the most important ones.

○ **Subject knowledge, technique and musicality:** Continue to practise and learn. Book yourself into mentor lessons with an experienced teacher if you feel you need to.

○ **Enthusiasm for teaching and students:** A passionate teacher is infectious. And students always learn more if they feel you like them and believe in them. Praise is important, so be generous (see Idea 5).

○ **Good planning:** Decide on a learning destination with your student and use this to develop a curriculum (see Idea 22).

○ **Good communication skills:** Listen to what your students say and don't do too much talking. Try to see parents and carers as an asset and communicate readily with them. Recognise that they love their child and communicate with this in mind.

○ **Business and organisation skills:** You need to prepare a timetable, invoice parents and carers, keep a record of receipts and do your tax return (see Ideas 94–100).

○ **Being adaptable:** As human beings our minds are programmed to confirm what we already believe (known as confirmation bias). This can affect the way we teach, making it ideological rather than based on the needs of the student. If they aren't learning, try another way and break the task into smaller steps. Ask yourself the question: 'How could I change, develop and improve?'

Taking it further...

Make a list of all your own music teachers' best characteristics and what you learnt from them. Use this information to inform your own teaching.

Top tip

You can never get it one hundred percent right as a teacher; if you think you do, then that could be a problem. Ensure that you actively engage in CPD (continuing professional development) – see Idea 87.

Avoid the 'mistake monitor' 7

"I cried after my lesson even though I am 40 years old. All my teacher did was criticise me. I felt totally demoralised!"

A common teaching method is to listen to students play something and then inform them of their errors. This can be crushing for students. Here are some ways to teach in which students discover for themselves how they can develop and grow.

Ways to avoid the mistake monitor:

○ **Properly prepare students before they embark on a new task:** Have you covered dotted rhythms in activities before? Do your students know the required notation? Make sure students understand what they are being asked to do.

○ **Use students' aural ability:** Ask them to listen to you playing two versions of the same piece of music, one correctly and the other including some of the students' errors. Ask them to describe which they feel is better and why?

○ **Encourage self-assessment through questions:** Ask your students to talk about all the good things about their performance but also if they had the opportunity to do it again, what they would do differently.

○ **Record them:** Due to the way we process information, it is impossible for students to hear with total accuracy what they are playing while they are playing it. They may not even register the number of false starts or repeated notes. Record them, and ask them to talk about what they hear.

Anecdote

One mother told me how her daughter had asked how she was doing with a particular section of music. Even though the mother heard several mistakes, she just encouraged. Her daughter then started self-assessing and even self-correcting without the mother having to mention any of the mistakes at all. The mother relayed how their relationship had improved since she no longer critiqued her child's playing.

8 The first lesson

"The first lesson is always an interesting one — no two students are alike!"

The first lesson is an important event; first impressions can lay the foundation for a productive musical partnership (or not). It is important to make music the heart of the lesson, and respond to the needs of the individual or group of students.

Here are some ideas to help you get started:

Welcome

It sounds really basic but 'smile' and do everything you can to put the student at ease. First impressions are important. This is hopefully the start of a long and musical journey.

Introduce yourself and get to know the student a little

If the lesson is a one-to-one, remember that this may be a very unusual thing for a child. It can also be very intense for an adult. Introducing yourself with a few interesting points can make the student feel more at ease, as can finding out a little bit about them.

Introduce the instrument

Some students can be really interested in how an instrument works. Demonstrate the instrument, show the strings, name the different parts, look at the patterns on the keyboard... Create some high and low sounds. Get the student to mark a steady pulse on the instrument, or simply with the voice or body percussion.

Top tip

It is important in the very beginning to train the student (and the parent if you are teaching a young child) on the correct posture and position of hands and arms when playing any instrument. Provide a good posture picture (even record on a mobile – with permission). Play a game of *Strictly technique and posture* (see Idea 31) when you and the parent mark the posture position out of 10, just like marking a dance. Children love to see actual cards with numbers on held up.

Play some musical games to help assess musical aptitude

There are lots of musical games involving pulse recognition, clapping back rhythms, singing the tonic, recognising high and low pitch (see *Music Express*, HarperCollins*Publishers*, for instance). This can give you a good idea of what musical foundation is there. Use flashcards and fun music apps.

Learn something to play

Make sure that music is at the heart of the lesson. Students like to leave the lesson being able to perform something and having something to work on. This can be taught by rote without notation.

Tutor book or no tutor book?

It's a good idea to take some time to select the right tutor book for a particular student, but you must remember that some children and especially their parents may want a book (or at least something) for their child to take away early on. You need to think very carefully about when is appropriate to introduce notation and a tutor. Sound before symbol is good practice, but it is also important to be guided by the student.

Taking it further...

Perform a piece of music on your instrument, if possible a special request. Adults in particular may enjoy hearing their teacher perform. It can be inspiring and also motivational.

Bonus idea

Young children love hearing their pet's and their own name. Incorporate either of these into a melody or rhyme for your student to sing or play (this can be just one note blown, two notes plucked, or if on a piano a few notes learnt by rote on the black keys).

9 A teaching style for very young students

"My youngest students love the puppets I bring into their lessons."

Teaching very young children requires a different and often a more imaginative teaching approach – from the way you speak to the children to the use of props!

Top tip

Many younger students love musical props – from finger puppets to puppets where they can mark the pulse. Boomwhackers and bongos are also great fun to explore rhythm. I've even used animal rubbers on the keyboard to identify different notes like a cat for C and a dog for D. Pencils can be great for practising bow holds too!

Bonus idea

Familiarise yourself with children's television aimed at this age group. It can model good practice and give you ideas of what language to use and which topics they may be interested in.

The very young have a limited attention span, respond to music physically and benefit hugely from singing and music games. Here are a few tips when working with young children:

- **Move to their physical level:** This means that you can maintain eye contact.

- **Keep instructions simple:** Language is beginning to develop at this age (though be aware that girls can be several months ahead of boys). However, children will have a limited vocabulary so for the most part won't understand words and phrases such as 'concentration', 'pay attention', 'that was very musical'. Speaking more slowly, and using shorter sentences, will help them better process what you are saying. Concentration levels are short and so snappy instructions work best.

- **Tone of voice:** Young children respond to a high level of animation and a gentle 'song-like' voice. You will notice that presenters on children's television programmes for this age group are highly animated and speak in a softer almost 'singing' voice. Instinctively you may find yourself doing this. It helps to maintain attention but also the 'warmth' in the voice can provide security for a very small child still working out their own place within the world. Don't do this forever, though.

Activities for the 10 very young

"Always have a bank of singing games up your sleeve."

Very young children enjoy learning music through play, repetition and most successfully through singing. Music can be a magical part of childhood that can become a lifelong love if the right materials are used. A whole body experience works well.

As noted in Idea 9, teaching very young students requires a slightly different approach. It is important to note that music in the early stages can bring a whole range of benefits to the child. Music doesn't just help the child develop musically; it can also help with language development, co-ordination and listening skills. Singing games, for example, can develop teamwork and practise physical and social skills.

Here are some musical approaches to explore with your youngest students:

○ Simplicity is best: Confidence is just developing with the very young. It's important that they enjoy much success. Provide simple material that can be successful with just the odd challenge.

○ Repetition: Children can enjoy repeated activities because they help them feel success and develop confidence – and the familiarity gives them a sense of safety.

○ Singing rhymes and games: Look out for the best materials, especially easy songs for children (visit Collins Music, Sing Up and Out of the Ark) but also for games that involve singing. Some favourite ones to start you off are: *Doggy Doggy where's your bone? Lucy Locket lost her pocket* and *The farmer's in his den*. These can easily be found online.

○ Instil a love of music: Remember you are setting the seeds for this child's future music education. Aim to instil a love for music and provide a good foundation for future learning, developing pulse, rhythm, pitch awareness and good intonation (tuning) in their singing voice.

Top tip

Introduce the 'musical pencil' – this can easily be incorporated into a music lesson by getting the student to use an imaginary musical pencil to mark the pulse, the phrases and high and low pitch.

Taking it further...

Useful organisations or materials that provide training for teaching music to young children include: The British Kodály Academy, Music Express Online, The Voices Foundation, The Dalcroze Society.

11 Young students (7–12 years)

"I love learning the guitar because I chose to and wasn't told to."

The average age a student starts to learn an instrument is aged 7–8. This is usually when the child can reasonably read written language. Here are some important ideas to be aware of when teaching students aged 7 to 12 years.

Research the development stages for this age range

Having an understanding where a student is developmentally will provide you with valuable information in your teaching. Talk to them each week, noting development and adjust your teaching accordingly.

Don't expect too much

The UK education system tends to organise learning in bite-sized chunks. Don't give your student too much to do, or make it too difficult (see Idea 74). They need to feel a sense of satisfaction in what they are doing. Learning an instrument is a slow process and children at this age like fast results.

Involve the parents/carers

Their daily support can be vital to help the student succeed. Do all you can to foster good relationships. Provide clear guidance on how they can support (rather than 'teach' their child). Explain that it is your job to teach and theirs to be their child's greatest fan.

Rewards and marking achievement

Children of this age group love to be rewarded for their efforts. Find out what works best for them – from stickers to performance opportunities (see Idea 75). Practice books provide a useful record of achievement.

Adolescent students 12

"Some teachers refer to teaching adolescents as a vexing frustration. I think of it as a vexing challenge!"

Teaching adolescent students with all the external pressures they face – school, exams, never mind growing up and all that entails – places challenges on your instrumental/singing teaching so you may need to be more creative. Here are some ideas how.

The external pressures on your adolescent students may mean practice taking a back seat at times. Don't niggle too much about this – accept it and ensure that lessons are always enjoyable regardless, but still have standards otherwise it will appear that you don't care.

○ **Explore composition:** Experiment with composing to help them create their own musical style.

○ **Ensembles:** Encourage your students to join or form an ensemble where they can meet like-minded teenagers.

○ **Give them responsibility:** Search online for topics related to their lesson – or, ask your students to explore online and then share their findings with you. A teacher who asks a student to show them how to do something is demonstrating a considerable sense of trust and confidence in the student's abilities.

○ **Have expectations of grown-up behaviour:** Many adolescents don't like to perform alongside unselfconscious younger children who have not yet got to the shy/hormonal stage. Arrange student concerts for just teenagers and theme it appropriately. Perhaps get them to organise the food and drink themselves – with some ground rules!

○ **Be flexible and approachable in planning:** Don't force the next exam on them just because it's there. If they really don't want to do exams, concentrate on playing for the quality and enjoyment of playing and performing. Students frequently come back later and *ask* to be allowed to take an exam.

Top tip

Many children find the transition to secondary school difficult. They will appreciate the continuity that their instrumental/singing lessons can provide, especially if the lessons provide an environment in which they feel valued and appreciated and where they have something to give.

Taking it further...

Explore different genres of music – try learning some traditional, jazz or pop music, but never lose quality. Teenagers are extremely discerning, so poor-quality pop music will get the same reaction as poor classical music.

13 Adult students

"Learn as if you were to live forever." Gandhi

Teaching an adult can require a different approach. Above all, you need to be flexible.

Here are some things to remember when teaching adults:

○ Establish why the adult wants lessons: What do they want to achieve? Do you feel you can help them achieve it? Keep expectations realistic – fingers, joints and the mind become less agile as we age.

○ Working as a facilitator: The adult's only aim maybe to be able to play a certain number of pieces. They may have no desire to learn any scales, music theory or participate in any creative activities. They may be open to other suggestions but also may not. You will have to decide whether you are comfortable with this.

○ Recognise an adult's need for context and explanations: Many adults feel the need to know *why* they are doing things as well as what they are doing.

○ Set realistic goals and be honest: Learning some instruments as an adult (especially from scratch), can be physically awkward. Be realistic with your student about what you think is possible. It may be best for them to try an alternative instrument with which they can enjoy more success.

○ Language: Teaching an adult will require a totally different approach from teaching a child. Great care needs to be taken with language used so as not to sound patronising.

Music is for everyone 14

"It is deeply rewarding working with my special needs and disabled children. They love music!"

Music can be very beneficial for students with learning difficulties or other disabilities such as hearing or sight impairments and cerebral palsy. Many organisations have experts available to help.

Here are some useful websites to get you started and to speed up the process of finding the information you need to help your students with SEND. Ideas 15 and 16 look at some specific learning difficulties in more detail. (All web addresses are correct at time of publication.)

British Dyslexia Association (BDA Music)

www.bdadyslexia.org.uk

This organisation has a music committee that provides support to teachers and learners. They also run a music and dyslexia qualification. Follow the link on their website to Educator, then Music and Dyslexia.

RNIB

rnib.org.uk

The RNIB support people with sight difficulties with all aspects of music-making, through individual advice and support.

Music and the Deaf

matd.org.uk

This organisation looks to enrich those with hearing loss through the experience of music.

Drake Music

drakemusic.org

https://theshortguidetoaccessiblemusic education.wordpress.com

This organisation uses new technology to open up the world of music to people with disabilities.

Top tip

It is worth taking the time to talk to the experts about what is best for your student. Some organisations such as the RNIB or the British Dyslexia Association run information days or even courses that you can attend.

Taking it further...

Find out about organisations in your local area too, e.g. **Yorkshire Association for Music and Special needs (yamsen.org.uk**). Your local music hub may have details.

15 Specific learning difficulties

"Music saved my son, and provided him with something he could be good at, despite his dyslexia."

Having a specific learning difficulty (SpLD) like dyslexia can affect music learning. However, if you understand the characteristics of SpLDs and some suitable steps that help to work with the difficulties, you can provide access to music learning.

Understand what SpLDs are and how common they are

They include: dyslexia, dyscalculia, dyspraxia, dysgraphia, Attention deficit (and hyperactivity) disorder (ADHD) and autistic spectrum disorders (ASDs), including Asperger's syndrome. According to the British Dyslexia Association, one in ten people have dyslexia.

How do I know if my student has an SpLD? What should I do?

Many students with SpLDs will *not* be assessed with these conditions. If you are working in a school, speak to the Head of Department or SENCO rather than speaking to the parent directly. Private practice teachers can gently refer parents to their child's school about assessment by an educational psychologist.

How to support visual difficulties

If a dyslexic student complains about the notes 'dancing' on the page, this can be something called visual stress (Irlam syndrome) which should be diagnosed by an optometrist (again refer to the SENCO, or parent if in private practice). Ways to help include enlarging music or putting it on coloured paper (alternatively, use coloured acetates over the top). Avoid white paper as it can cause glare.

Expert help

The British Dyslexia Association provides teaching materials and courses for music teachers working with dyslexic students (see Idea 14).

Top tip

If you suspect your student has a difficulty (even without an assessment) teach them in a way suitable for the condition anyway.

Taking it further...

When providing text, use a font that is clear for students with dyslexia, like a large sans-serif font. Avoid Times New Roman and handwritten text.

SpLD memory boosters

"Following the same lesson structure each week really helps."

Working memory and short-term memory are both affected by SpLDs, whereas the long-term memory is not. Use the following tools and teaching strategies to help overcome these problems for your students.

Decoding information

This can be challenging for a student with an SpLD, due to processing problems (working memory).

○ Use highlighter pens to mark important information. Colour-code their music, making each note a different colour (the late Margaret Hubicki used the colours of the rainbow in her colour staff method). Highlight all the sharps, flats and naturals – using different colours for each.

Helping with problems with short-term and working memory

○ Find ways to make organisation easier: create a personal timetable for lessons and if possible organise the lesson for the same time each week; add reminders of what to practise on their mobile phone; create one folder that includes all their music (following photocopying guidelines for disabilities).

○ Be understanding if students are late or forget lessons – provide sticky notes to write reminders.

Use appropriate teaching methods

○ Use a structured approach, as this can help with memory problems.

○ Use multi-sensory teaching methods – mainly sight, hearing and touch (see Idea 69).

○ Make things memorable through either personal association (perhaps a rhyme made up by the student to learn a scale) or something so whacky it's hard to forget.

○ Embedding – repeat things over and over to get them into the student's long-term memory (which is not affected by their SpLD).

○ Use approaches like Kodály (see Idea 67), Dalcroze (see Ideas 60–61) and Suzuki (see Idea 64).

> **Top tip**
>
> Find ways to boost your student's self esteem by giving *specific* praise (so it's very clear and authentic). Students with spLDs can take longer to complete tasks resulting in tiredness, anxiety/stress; in some cases this can lead to low self-esteem.

17 Challenging students?

"Some students prefer to follow their own agenda. Go with it and expand."

Students who find (or make) situations 'challenging' usually have another agenda that is nothing to do with their music. If you can see the 'challenge' as finding a way to try and lift them out of their doldrums by giving them appropriate activities, you should be able to get them back on track.

Explore these ideas:

○ Choice of repertoire: Work hard at finding the right repertoire for these students. Discuss their ideal choice and try to find something close that will appeal.

○ Individual choice: If they don't like the repertoire, suggest different ways in which they can help select the repertoire, e.g. set them the task of researching for homework, or give them the task of composing their own piece for them as an individual or a group to learn.

○ Responsible task: In group lessons, make them feel important by giving them a responsible task to do – they will usually be particularly good at organising the other students!

○ Rewards: If they have stayed on task, allow them to choose the repertoire for the following week's lesson. Don't be afraid of withdrawing that privilege of choice if they have not successfully stayed on task – they can wait another week.

Top tip
We all like compliments and usually work better for praise rather than criticism. Find something to praise at the beginning and end of every lesson – it doesn't have to be to do with music or practice (it could just be a new hairstyle!).

○ Assisting other students: Ask them to assist with some of the other students. That way, even if they can't play the piece themselves, they will have to work out strategies for how to go about playing it so that the rest of the group can respond. They will be learning from this themselves as they help others.

○ Organisational jobs: Give organisational jobs to promote a feeling of self-worth – putting up stands, arranging chairs, etc.

○ Say something positive: *Always* find something good to say – congratulate them on a football team result, notice if they have remembered their music, etc.

Talented students

"The word 'musical' is often used, but yet is very difficult to define accurately!"

'Gifted and talented' is a term used in schools to describe students who have the potential to develop significantly beyond what is expected for their age. 'Gifted' refers to a child who has abilities in one or more academic subjects, such as English or maths. 'Talented' refers to a child who has skills in a practical area such as music, sport or art.

There is never a sure way of identifying talent, because every young musician is different. Some start slowly and appear to be progressing steadily and then flourish; others take off at vast speed with huge expectations but then hit a brick wall. Thankfully there are some in the middle.

Here are some thoughts on identifying and teaching talented students.

● Signs of musical talent can be numerous (e.g. associating movement and emotions in music), but be wary of making assumptions. Having perfect pitch does not mean a student will play perfectly in tune!

● Talented students need plenty of challenges and stimulation. Just working through the grades is unlikely to be enough – seriously talented students may well have achieved Grade 8 by the time they reach the age of 10 but that is only really the start of the ladder.

● Performance opportunities are a must and, as well as solos, these might include attending one of our NYMOs (National Youth Music Organisations, e.g. National Youth Orchestra, National Youth Choirs, National Youth Jazz Collective, etc.) as well as courses such as Pro Corda chamber music and National Youth Wind Ensemble, etc.

● If your student is champing at the bit, it may be the time to steer them towards specialist music education, either through the Junior Conservatoires and Centres for Advanced Training or the Specialist Music Schools. All of these have support from the DfE's *Music and Dance Scheme* with the possibility of means-tested grant assistance. If in doubt, ask them for advice.

Top tip

Sometimes being 'identified' as talented can bring expectations which may be difficult to achieve. Be aware of this potential difficulty for your students.

19 Lesson plan – individual lesson

"I believe my teaching has been successful when my students don't need me any more."

Planning lessons should always look to the future (both the short term and the long term) as well as being responsive to what has happened in the past week's practice. This sample lesson plan is for an individual lesson and Idea 20 is for more than one student. However, the musical ideas within them can be used in any teaching situation.

This sample lesson plan is based on an individual violin lesson but can be easily adapted to different instruments/the voice.

Welcome

Greet the student and have a quick catch-up on how things are going whilst getting instruments and music sorted.

Tuning up

Always encourage the student to do as much of this as possible as they progress. Early on they can play the open strings (long bows to make a good sound) while you adjust the pegs, then gradually this can change to them moving the pegs/adjusters themselves. Ask questions, such as: 'Do you think it's too high/too low?', rather than just telling them.

Warming up

Include technical exercises and games, e.g.

● Play 'copycat phrases': you play a phrase and the student copies back – change your position so that the student can't always see you and therefore has to do it by ear.

● Over time, gradually move on to a more 'question and answer' style and then even more improvising.

Bonus idea

If concentration is lapsing at any point in the lesson, do something completely different for a few moments, such as bouncing a ball to feel the weight of the beat or stepping the rhythm of a small section and 'writing' it out using flashcards. Have an armoury of activities like this for every lesson.

● Include body warm-ups: shoulder circles, arm swings, 'finger press-ups', bendy knees, etc.

Technique

Spend some time on technique. As your student progresses, introduce a technical passage or study to focus on a specific aspect of technique.

Repertoire

● Invite the student to play through their first piece. Try not to stop them if there's a slip – allow the fluency to develop and remember for later.

● Discuss any difficulties and work on small sections. Ask the student to think of ways to tackle a tricky bit and then give more strategies for aiding practice of specific problems.

● If possible, play a small section with accompaniment – either single line or piano. Discuss the difference the harmonic sense makes to the shaping.

● Play through a second piece, but look at this from the 'overall' perspective of structure and shape rather than the nitty-gritty of technique, thereby developing different aspects and possibilities from different pieces.

● If there are more pieces that have been practised, try to find time to hear at least a little bit so that the student never thinks their practice has been wasted.

Finish

Finish with a really good play – even if it's just a small section – so that progress can be felt and they take away a sense of achievement.

Make a record in their and your notebook

Note things to work on in their notebook. Note thoughts for the future (both short term and longer term) in your notebook.

Top tip

When using technical exercises or studies, I have found technical passages that are no more than half a page long, giving a short concentration on a particular aspect (e.g. a bowing technique) to be most effective. Depending on your individual student (and time), you may choose to explore three such exercises in a lesson.

Taking it further...

Some studies have a really good second part. These are really useful tools as they fulfil many uses, e.g. developing a good tone (through trying to emulate the teacher's tone); developing fluency in sight reading or playing passages without stopping; developing a technical idea alongside you, so seeing as well as thinking and listening.

20 Lesson plan – more than one student

"I try to make every lesson musical, memorable and enjoyable."

This idea sits alongside Idea 19. It provides an outline for a lesson plan based on a small group lesson.

Welcome and review the past week's practice

Greet the students with a smile and positive comments and discuss highs/lows over the week and allow them time to give feedback on anything they had been asked to research.

Tuning and warming up

Short technical tasks appropriate for the specific instrument or voice (see also Idea 19). Introduce a well-known short piece played with an accompaniment to ensure the pulse is maintained.

Repertoire

❍ Invite the students to perform the piece they have been practising.

❍ Give some creative activities to enable the students to self-correct, e.g. if the pulse wasn't maintained, demonstrate the piece and encourage them to 'walk' the pulse; do 'spot the difference' activities.

❍ Look at a new piece, sight-read some of it and discuss researching more about it.

❍ Discuss what to practise and provide different strategies for this.

Creative activities

Explore improvisation, composing or playing by ear activities based on the new repertoire.

Set a practice goal

What does each student want to achieve in the week ahead? Provide incentives.

Finish

Praise! Always focus on the positive and discuss opportunities for learning rather than 'what went wrong!'

Taking it further...

Explore the ingredients of a piece: background, key (use scales and arpeggios); structure; style/period; scale and arpeggio patterns; cadences. Explain the Italian terms. Use aural activities to explore the music further.

Thinking outside the box! 21

"I love art and I love music, but I never realised they were connected!"

Teaching an instrument is only a small part of music and music is only a part of the ingenuity and artistry that exist in all our daily lives, so we should frequently look for ideas and connections 'outside the box'.

Here are some creative ideas to explore with your students, thinking 'outside the box'!

Explore the history of your instrument

● How was it originally made?

● Would it have sounded the same then as it does now?

● How is the sound affected now?

● What else was being made/played at the same time?

● Which instruments would have been played together?

Explore other artistic happenings at the time of composition of the pieces being studied

● What was the architecture of the time like?

● Can you find some pictures of buildings of the time on the internet?

● Can you find some pictures by artists of the time?

● What was happening in the dance world at the time? Try and find examples of dances and try them out (e.g. Baroque dance can be hugely enlightening with regard to the study of Baroque music).

● Explore some literature of the period being studied and then ally this to the artwork and music of the time.

Encourage your students to get creative

● Ask your students to paint a picture or write a story and then compose their own, stylistic piece about it or inspired by it.

Anecdote

I was very lucky once to be invited to a concert in a private house where the walls were decked (often three deep) with some of the finest examples of British art. Listening to a wonderful string quartet playing, whilst having my imagination tapped by these fabulous pictures, awakened a whole new array of senses thanks to the connections between these two great art forms.

22 Planning a curriculum

"Planning your own curriculum means it will be more specific to your needs and more likely to remain a useful resource."

There is no national curriculum for instrumental music. Various bodies have gone some way towards helping and advising on a curriculum (see Taking it further), but it will be best for you if you are able to plan your own.

Be careful not to confuse curriculum with syllabus. The syllabus is likely to be a list of pieces for a specific level, such as a grade exam, whereas your curriculum looks at the learning picture over a wider span of time. Here are some pointers to get you started:

○ Choose a number of stages: Choose a number of stages that are appropriate for your teaching (e.g. Years 3–4, GCSE performance, etc.)

○ Set short- and long-term goals: Work out the short- and long-term goals for each of these stages (e.g. learn about a sense of pulse and rhythmic notation in 2/4 and 4/4; discover the structures of some simple Baroque pieces).

○ Decide on a time span: Decide where you want this process to get to and how long would be your ideal learning time for each goal.

○ SEND students: Remember that SEND students may need longer to reach their goals (see Ideas 15–16).

○ Stick to broad descriptions and ideas: Leave specific pieces to the syllabus but have focused goals to achieve at each stage. Don't make it too wordy – bullet points are fine, and try to confine your ideas for each stage to only one page, maximum!

○ Flesh it out: Once you are happy with the broad outline of your curriculum, flesh it out with some syllabus ideas.

Taking it further...

Although *A Common Approach* (2002) is now a little aged, it was the fullest, in-depth analysis for instrumental teaching and is a useful reference as much still applies today.

Sample curriculum plan

"I'm constantly worried I may have missed something."

Having a handy form for each student can be a useful planning tool to ensure you are covering everything systematically.

	Details (include changes if required due to student feedback)	Date to be covered (give term/year details)
Technical Scales and arpeggios and also instrument-specific techniques, e.g. vibrato, muting, stopping, pedalling		
Repertoire Classical – *all* periods; jazz; popular; student choice		
Aural Pulse and time signature; identifying dynamics, articulation and tempo; rhythm and melodic memory; style and period recognition; recognising changes in pitch and rhythm in a melody; sight singing; harmony intervals/chords.		
Sight-reading skills Intervals, keys, time signatures, rhythm patterns, style of music.		
Musicianship Composing, improvisation, playing by ear.		
Theory What grade if appropriate are you going to cover?		
Practice strategies for independent learning		
Other		

Top tip

Be flexible about whether and how often and you complete a curriculum planning form. For some students it is far better to have no agenda and to move where their learning naturally takes them. For other students who are working towards an examination or need to get a to a certain level for a scholarship or access to music college/university, a plan can be pretty essential. And, if you use a plan, be willing to change with the needs of your students.

24 Systematic and reinforced teaching

"Teach the easy before the difficult." (Mrs Curwen's maxims)

Systematic teaching is about following a logical process. Reinforced teaching is where the same concept is taught in different ways and in different contexts.

This idea suggests ways to teach a piece of music in a systematic and reinforced way.

○ **Title:** From the title of the piece, what does a student think the music will sound like? Perform the piece of music to the student (or listen to a recording) and ask them to describe it in words (e.g. 'bouncy', 'happy', 'spooky', etc.).

○ **Pulse:** Mark the pulse (the heartbeat) either by tapping heart shapes on a page, clapping, using claves or counting. Work out which way is best for your student.

○ **Rhythm:** Explore the rhythms in the piece, firstly through clapping games in which the student copies you. Then, once the rhythm is accurately copied aurally, provide the notation for the student (sound before symbol). Can the student then perform the rhythms taken from the piece on flashcards or in small sections?

○ **Pitch:** Can the student listen to the melody line of the music and mark the shape of it in terms of high and low as they listen (doing it simply using a finger in the air or by following the music)? Can the student spot any scale or arpeggio patterns or any repeated passages or sequences?

○ **Interpretation:** Discuss your interpretation of the piece. Decide on the tempo (use the markings). Identify the phrase marks and articulation (perhaps use physical gestures of moving the arm in line with the phrase, or highlight articulation on the music with a marker). Dynamics can be marked on the music using colours, with the student selecting the colours, or the student could internalise the dynamics through listening.

Top tip

When reinforcing learning, try to use 'whacky' ways to make it more memorable, e.g. a funny, dramatic story or rhyme. One of my students made up a fantastic rhyme to remember their note names that included their granny and bogies!

Repertoire diary

"Students should always have at least something ready for if they need to perform."

A repertoire diary provides a historical document of a student's instrumental lessons that they can look back at for many years to come. It can be a valuable document packed with useful information and reminders of music that has been enjoyed.

Issue your student with a repertoire diary when they first start lessons. Explain that they can use this for as long as they want to. Explain its uses, e.g. finding a piece to play at a concert; using it to help with music lessons in school; giving background information that can be used in music exams, especially in aural tests and a viva (describing the style of music); and most importantly, recording information about music they have enjoyed or even loved playing.

How to make a repertoire diary

Create a notebook or file with three sections as follows:

Tutor book section

The student provides details of what pieces they are enjoying in their tutor book and why.

Manuscript paper section

This is for students' 'own compositions' – encourage students in the early stages to compose simply using the few notes they have learnt.

Repertoire section

The student makes a note on each piece of repertoire they play. This should include:

- the name of the piece and the composer

- a description of the character of the music

- the style of the music (include period, e.g. Baroque, Classical, etc.)

- background information on the composer if possible

- interesting information about the piece, e.g. features of the music

- whether the student likes it

- any other music composed by the composer that the student has found on YouTube or heard performed and would like to play.

26 Report-writing

"I have to write so many of these, it's good to have a plan!"

A yearly report can sometimes be one of the opportunities to communicate with parents, especially if working in a school. Parents want a quick summary but also appreciate some kind of indication that you really understand their child. Time taken doing a good report can be good business sense.

Top tip

Try to write the report in a way that you would want to read it if written about yourself (or your own child). Focus on the positive and talk about critical elements in a constructive way, e.g. 'Ellie is beginning to practise effectively.' Make sure there are no surprises in there – issues should have been dealt with during the course of the lessons, not left to the report.

Anecdote 🗩

When writing my reports, I have in mind the objective of encouraging the student to carry on learning. I praise their achievement and hopefully give them a belief that they can achieve continually as we work together in the future.

This sample report plan can be adapted to suit your students' needs and form part of a school music department or music hub reporting policy.

Topics	Details
Technique Repertoire Musicianship Reading Theory Posture Practice	
Exams Concert Festival details	
General comment	
Targets for next term	
Achievement (provide a motivational sentence celebrating the student)	

Pulse and rhythm

"If the sense of pulse is secure, rhythm is just the patterns in the boxes."

Build up the sense of pulse and rhythm from the very beginning using fun activities that develop the students' own inner pulse.

Note value flashcards

Make a set of simple note value flashcards (at least eight of each note value) by drawing notes with a thick felt-tip pen on pieces of card. For notes of less value than a crotchet, each card should add up to a crotchet (e.g. two quavers, four semiquavers). Use the flashcards frequently – a small part of every lesson – so pulse and rhythm become second nature not something 'scary'.

Activities

◗ Use simple activities to mark the pulse, e.g. walking around the room, tapping knees, chanting a word rhythm in time to the pulse, etc.

◗ Make a game of moving in time with the pulse while playing a piece (e.g. marching on the spot), or, for keyboard players, move the rhythm of one hand while singing the part of the other hand.

◗ Play a sub-division game – you tap crotchets whilst the student taps quavers; when you call, 'Swap!', you swap parts, without a gap! Gradually add more rhythm patterns as confidence grows.

◗ Encourage students to demonstrate rhythm with their feet, if enough room – full body movement *feels* the sense of pulse much more than clapping (see Ideas 32 and 60).

◗ Play a simple two-bar melody and ask students to demonstrate the rhythmic pattern with their feet. Repeat a few times. Then, give them the flashcards and ask them to 'write' the rhythm.

◗ Use flashcards to 'write' the rhythm pattern of a new piece; ask students to demonstrate the rhythm with their feet to experience the pulse and rhythm before adding notes.

Top tip

When making note value flashcards, don't use the same colour card for each note value – otherwise students can learn to associate the colour with the note value instead of reading the actual note.

Top tip

Don't progress rhythm too quickly – use crotchets and quavers only to start with and add another card only when this is secure.

28 Notation games

"My students love games — all games!"

Most students love playing a game to learn notes or rhythm patterns – it is so much better than sitting and 'learning' notes!

Here are some ideas of notation games to play with your students.

Flashcards (see Idea 27)

Always remember to start simple and increase one thing at a time, e.g.

● Show four crotchet cards and ask your student to demonstrate the rhythm with their feet.

● Change one crotchet to two quavers and ask the student to demonstrate that rhythm.

● Change another note value card.

Bonus idea

Before deciding to 'teach notation', ask yourself what it is the student needs to know: do they need to know the letter name or is it sufficient to know where the note is on the instrument?

Taking it further...

There are masses of notation games online that can give more games to play. Just be wary of ones that teach a note name without any relation to an instrument.

Stave jumping

'Draw' a stave on the floor using coloured tape. Students jump quickly from one note to the next as you call the letter name. They can take turns to be caller (but they have to know if it's the right note). Develop this gradually, e.g.

● Jump a three-note pattern, then play it or sing it.

● Using the floor stave, point out where the notes are by step or 'skips' as this helps to develop the idea of patterns, which is a much quicker way of reading than note-names.

Stave storyboard

Make up a story in which missing words are 'spelt' out by notes on the stave – use a magnetic board or magnetic whiteboard with staves on, if possible. For example:

James went to ___ ___ ___ .

You can get much more variety if you use some letters interspersed, e.g.

It was an _A_ v _E_ r _A_ _G_ _E_ day.

"I practise in front of a large mirror — it really helps!"

Developing good posture in our students requires constant reminders in order to create habits that allow the body to use itself successfully and freely. Remember that the 'natural' posture that has developed in some children (and adults) is rarely the best.

Good posture involves training your body to stand, walk, sit and lie in positions where the least strain is placed on supporting muscles and ligaments during movement or weight-bearing activities.

Here are some hints and tips to get you started. You might also like to play Strictly technique and posture (see Idea 31).

○ **Raise awareness:** Most of us are unaware of our poor posture habits, so raising awareness is the first move.

○ **Use a mirror:** Use a mirror to check that the body is being used in a balanced, free way, and persuade students to use a mirror when practising at home (you might need to persuade parents to get one placed in a suitable position).

○ **Learn how best to hold the instrument:** Few instruments are played or held in a 'natural' position so it is important to learn the best use of a balanced muscular hold that works without tension.

○ **Use a skeleton:** Borrowing a skeleton from a science teacher can help students to see how the body structure works.

Top tip

Try sitting on a large ball (or if standing, stand on a small trampoline) – if you haven't got a large exercise ball, try using a football-sized ball on a low stool. An immediate effect is that the feet need to be well placed to help balance (no curling around the chair leg!). The freedom of movement is increased and there is usually an increase in the level of sound produced because everything is more relaxed.

Taking it further...

An awareness and study of techniques such as the Alexander Technique, the Feldenkrais method and Pilates all help to improve postural control – for students and teachers.

30 Good technique from the start

"An awareness of how the body works to best effect will help develop a sound and reliable technique."

As a teacher, you may have found yourself repairing techniques that have been allowed to slip in to bad practice. This can be avoided if you raise awareness from the start about what is actually going on both with the player and the instrument.

Top tip

Part of the development process must include the player learning what to do to make their instrument work at its best. Just managing to play the notes will not create a lasting technique.

Taking it further...

Play the 'Sort me out' game in which the student corrects your technique – deliberately use bad posture, for example, and ask your student to correct it. Be prepared for them to pick up on something you thought you had corrected!

Here are some ideas for helping your students develop a good technique from the start:

○ Start slowly: At the beginning, don't try to cover too much ground too quickly. It is much better to play two notes exquisitely than ten notes badly. It is then up to you to make those two exquisite notes sound exciting by perhaps adding accompaniment, improvising around them, etc.

○ Checklist: Develop a checklist of good practice (e.g. checking posture, right and left hand positions, etc.). If you keep this in the front of the student's notebook, you can expand on it when and where appropriate.

○ Breathing: Even for an instrument that doesn't 'require' breath, it is a vital tool to develop the feeling of shapes and phrases. For example, encouraging pianists to breathe as if singing the phrases greatly helps their playing have shape and style.

○ Mirror: Have a mirror in teaching rooms so that students can see for themselves what things look like; this can hugely increase the speed of their understanding and awareness.

Strictly technique 31 and posture

"Technique and posture go hand in hand..."

Good posture is a basic foundation for ensuring good technique on any instrument and preventing injuries. Playing games that encourage good practice from the beginning can be motivational and effective for younger students. Strictly technique and posture is a fun game to get you started!

○ **Training:** Provide your student with a picture, YouTube video or detailed instructions on the correct posture for playing their instrument.

○ **Score cards:** Have a set of numbers 5 to 10 (*Strictly Come Dancing* style) to hold up to mark your student out of 10 on how good their posture is.

○ **Scoring:** Mark their posture at intervals during the lesson (no more than three times) to encourage the student to develop good posture habits. Explain to the student the need for good posture and what physical problems can occur with poor posture.

○ **Scoreboard:** Record their scores in their practice books and encourage them to assess their own posture at home.

Taking it further...

Be aware of what injuries can be caused by poor posture and technique on your instrument. A useful starting place is the British Association for Performing Arts Medicine (BAPAM).

Bonus idea

Encourage students to look in a mirror or film themselves at home to check things like correct piano stool height and position, general posture, bow hold, embouchure, etc.

Anecdote

I was having difficulty improving the posture of a young violin student so asked him to record his practice. All became clear when I saw he had the music on his bed and was bending over to be able to see it!

32 Singing warm-ups

"Singing is like marathon–running in miniature!"

Singing without warming up can be as damaging as running a race without warming up; the voice and body need to be ready to sing well so that vocal chords aren't strained, breathing comes more easily, and singing can be the pleasure it is meant to be. Follow the advice below for a STAPLE diet for singing.

The singing mnemonic STAPLE stands for: Stamina, Tone/Tonality, Agility, Pitch, Looseness, Energy:

STAMINA

Persuade your students to practise this breathing exercise regularly every day if only for a few minutes (it can be done while walking to school!):

● Breathe *in* for three (1, 2, 3) and *out* for four (1, 2, 3, 4), then *in* for four; *out for* five, continuing to *in* for seven; *out* for eight.

● Gradually include sounds on the out breaths, e.g. Pa, pa, pa; Mum, Mum, Mum, etc.

TONE/TONALITY

Sing long sounds using a variety of vowel sounds and consonants. You are aiming for a consistent, sustained tone throughout the length of the note.

AGILITY

Use some spoken tongue twisters (e.g. *Peter Piper picked a peck of pickled pepper*) as well as some sung ones (e.g. sing to the tune of *William Tell*: 'mind your mum, mind your mum, mind your mum, mum, mum'; or 'diss your dad', 'touch your toes', etc.). You or your students can invent more!

Top tip

Remember that breathing in should involve the whole ribcage – students should feel the breath expanding and filling the back and lower ribcage (it's often easier to try the breathing warm-up lying on the floor).

PITCH

○ **Call and response:** Sing simple two-bar melodies for your students to copy.

○ **Pitching intervals:** Sing simple intervals for your students to copy.

○ **Sol-fa:** The Kodály method of teaching singing using solfa names can be an excellent way to improve intonation (tuning), see Idea 67.

LOOSENESS

It is important to develop looseness of voice and body. Try these ideas:

○ **Sink plunger:** Sing patterns (slowly), allowing the voice to slide up and down in a glissando, e.g. C – G – C; D – A – D, etc.

○ **Sink plunger with actions:** Add actions synchronised with the notes, e.g. hands flop down to the toes and bounce up to stretch over the head.

○ **Jumps:** Jump twice as though you are catching a basketball, land with flexed knees.

○ **Plant yourself:** Plant yourself, with arms by your side as if you are holding two big shopping bags.

○ **Shoulder circles:** Place hands on shoulders and draw circles with your elbows, remembering to change the direction.

○ **Shoulder lifts:** Lift shoulders up-up-up, then roll backwards and down-down-down.

○ **Shake out:** Shake the arms, shake the legs, shake the body all over.

ENERGY

○ Play rhythm warm-ups, such as chanting rhythm flashcards, to develop both energy responses and rhythmic reading.

○ Body percussion and clapping games use the whole body and encourage energetic actions and reactions.

Taking it further...

Find a range of rounds, partner songs and singing games that can be used as part of the warm-up. There are several public domain ones to explore, e.g. I love the flowers; Bella Mamma; Si Si Si, Viva la Musica (rounds); Swing low, When the Saints and I'm going to sing, sing, sing together; and Step back baby and Chick Hanka (partner songs). There are lots of singing games online.

33 Sensational scales

"Scales can be a little like Marmite™ — some love them and some hate them!"

A full range of teaching tips and tricks is needed to help students learn their scales. It is an ongoing thing, and should be done as part of any musician's regular practice – not just when they have an exam. An individual learning approach is essential – if at first they don't succeed, provide them with an alternative strategy.

Here is an ABC guide to learning sensational scales!

A is for aural sense

First things first: the student needs to be able to hear what the correct scale should sound like. Try playing some of the modes, such as the Dorian mode (D E F G A B C D) and invite the student to add notes to turn this into the major scale and, when appropriate, the harmonic minor scale and melodic minor scale. Ask them to sing back the final discovered scales.

B is for break the learning down

Start with the first five notes of the scale (the *EastEnders* theme tune) and ask the student to play this by ear starting on different notes. Finally add in the last two notes and the tonic.

C is for circle of fifths

This is an excellent visual tool for a student to work from (see Idea 44), gradually working through all the major and minor scales systematically.

D is for doing activities

Here are some example 'doing activities':

● Chant the scale doing the fingering if appropriate.

● Ask the student to draw pictures that help them remember the sharps and flats in a scale (e.g. D major – Fish [F#] and Chips [C#]).

● Provide pictures of the keyboard/ fingerboard/fretboard/keys and holes and ask the student to highlight the notes to be played.

● Practise scales in different rhythms (instruments other than keyboard can perform a short rhythm pattern on each note of the scale).

● Use scales as a warm-up, varying dynamics and articulation (perhaps playing the scale of the key the repertoire is written in).

● Encourage improvisation with different scales for key sense.

● Invite students to record to see how well they are doing.

E is for eyes on notation

Is your student aware of the patterns they are playing, watching the scale notation as they play (feeling the fingering linking with the patterns)?

F is for fingers

Fingers need training the right way from the start. It is important for students to understand the different fingering patterns for their instrument. Start slowly so they are learnt correctly.

G is for go over and over them

Rehearsing over and over will get the notes and the fingering into the long-term memory – but remember to start slowly.

Bonus idea

Provide or ask your students to make scale pots. List all the scales, arpeggios and broken chords on a piece of card, then cut it up so each one is separate. Put them in a pot. Students pick a card; once they can play the scale perfectly they transfer it into a 'learnt' pot; if not perfect it goes back into the original pot. Once all have been transferred, start the process again.

34 Developing musical style

"Style can be developed through gesture and gesture can help to develop a style."

Once you progress past notes and rhythms, it is important to understand what makes the music special and stylish. As Artur Schnabel said, 'The notes I handle no better than many pianists. But the pauses between the notes – ah, that is where the art resides.'

Listening

If a student has not heard or realised about musical style then the first step needs to be to develop a series of listening projects. YouTube is a valuable tool for this.

❍ Ask students to listen to three different YouTube clips of a piece (it doesn't have to be their own instrument) and identify:

▸ Which one did they like best?

▸ Why?

▸ Was it to do with what they heard or what they saw?

▸ How might their listening affect how they are playing?

❍ From this, move on to pieces from different periods and discuss the differences in style.

Taking it further...

Expand the listening a little more each month to different styles and periods and then seek out the different compositional techniques – a little at a time.

Top tip

A general sense of inquisitiveness about how the music came to be can open the active mind to explore more.

Music animation machine (musanim.com)

Stephen Malinowski has created animated music scores which are worthwhile exploring. They can really help students to understand how the music 'works' as the eye is lead through the musical structure which, in turn, feeds thoughts about how to develop the style in our own playing.

Singing

Stress the importance, and do lots, of singing of music – this is the natural way to shape music; the rise and fall being easier to do with the voice, as you *have* to take breaths, which gives the natural phrase shaping.

"A painter paints pictures on canvas. But musicians paint their pictures on silence." Leopold Stokowski

Instilling the idea of beautiful phrasing at an early age can make even the very beginner into a real musician.

Explore some of these ideas with your students:

○ **Listen and draw:** Listen to a short piece of music, drawing the shape of the phrases in the air – simple folk songs are ideal. Notice that the shape of your drawn phrase is probably a curved line – very much like the phrase marks in the music.

○ **Musical sentences:** The words of the song may also help to give phrasing ideas – as can likening music phrases to sentences, commas, etc.

○ **Rounding off notes:** Practise making *f* then suddenly *p* sounds to get a feeling for really rounding off notes at the ends of phrases.

○ **Shapes and patterns:** Look for shapes and patterns within a phrase, particularly ones that help the build up or down, such as sequences.

○ **Cadence shapes:** Listen for the harmony creating phrase shapes in a piece of music – usually with a cadence – and notice how long each phrase is. How can you vary the sounds of each phrase to help form a whole picture?

○ **Phrase lengths:** Although four-bar phrases are the most common, pieces frequently have variations of one-, two-, four- and eight-bar phrases quite regularly. You can also find examples of three-bar phrases in some quite early music. Try exploring some of the Bartók/ Kodály folk song collections – there are some interesting phrase lengths there!

○ **Body movements:** Use the body to mimic the phrasing of a piece – allow the gestures to rise and fall in the same way a phrase mark would.

Top tip

Very light, soft silk scarves can be used to show phrases and really demonstrate the different delicateness of shorter/longer phrase patterns most beautifully.

36 Listening

"The art of listening needs a bit of encouragement!"

With all the music being produced as background noise in our surroundings (in the supermarket, in cars, people 'plugged into' their MP3 player, etc.), students often need a bit of help to train their ears to really listen to and hear sounds.

Here are some ideas to help develop your students' true listening skills.

- **Spot the difference – phrases game:** Play a game in which you play a phrase, then repeat it but with a change – can the student identify the difference?
- **Spot the difference – notation game:** Try the same game as above, but giving your student the music. You play a phrase but with a wrong note or rhythm – the student has to identify which note was wrong and why. Gradually expand this to a short piece in which you ask them to identify the four things you did that were different from the printed music (e.g. dynamics, pitch, rhythm, tempo, etc.)
- **Make a recording:** Record your student's playing and ask them to assess the playback. Be wary of filming for safeguarding reasons (you would need to ensure you have parental permission and preferably ask parents to be present).
- **Three versions game:** Play your student three different versions of the same music. Ask them to identify what they like best/least about each performance and why. This can work really well if you can use a recording of their own playing and two others – can they identify their own playing?

Bonus idea

Set your student the task of recording (they can use their mobile phones) three different sound bites (10–20 seconds duration). They could be outside (e.g. birdsong or traffic) or inside (e.g. recorded music playing in a shopping centre or sounds at school, etc.) What do they hear?

Anecdote

The word 'listen' contains the same letters as 'silent'!

Starting points for developing musicianship

"Sometimes you need a little time to lay some musical foundations at the start."

It is always worth exploring a student's general musicianship early on. Students who have not been exposed to as much music previously may need a little time spent building some musical foundations at the start.

Use the ideas below to explore your student's musical starting point so you can build from there:

○ **Rhythm patterns:** Clap and use body percussion to give some rhythm patterns for your student to copy. If this is easy, move on to more of a question and answer type response. Do they pick them up quickly?

○ **Copy singing:** Play or sing some short phrases for your student to copy (see Top tip). Start simply – perhaps only three notes and *gradually* add in more and more. If it gets too hard, go back a couple of steps so you end on success.

○ **Listening exercise:** Play some music – either yourself or a recording – and invite the student to explain what they hear. Encourage them to think imaginatively, e.g. does it tell a story? Does it paint a picture? Can they imagine different splashes of colour?

○ **Move to the music:** Improvise some music for them to move to – make big differences between high and low pitch and loud and soft sounds and ask them to interpret the differences with their movements.

Top tip

A beginner who doesn't sing in tune has probably never used their vocal chords before and so not realised the variations they are able to make. Encourage them to sing something to you and then use that same area of pitch to make up simple songs to sing. Sing regularly in that note range with them and then expand the range gradually.

38 Making music the heart of each lesson

"Less talking, more music!"

Students learn a great deal from doing, especially at younger ages when language and listening skills are just developing.

Explore some of these ideas for developing musical learning:

Top tip

Give your students a choice of music to play – they could vote (giving marks out of 10) on what piece they want to study. When students are involved in repertoire selection, I've found they are more likely to practise it!

Bonus idea

Set your student the task of finding music themselves to learn. Be specific with the requirements, e.g. tell them how long it should be (e.g. one page); what key it should be in; what it needs to develop in their playing… You can expand this to 'one plus one' where you pick a piece and then they pick a piece.

Developing aural skills

When learning new repertoire, use the pieces to develop aural skills (to identify pulse, rhythm, pitch, melody, structure, texture, timbre, tempo, dynamics and articulation), e.g:

○ **Pitch:** Exploring high and low notes on the instrument

○ **Pulse:** Marking the pulse of a piece through clapping or playing a percussion instrument

○ **Scales:** Finding and then playing scale passages in the music

○ **Structure:** Performing the music to identify the structure.

Listening to pieces in their original context

Students often play arrangements of pieces originally written for a different instrument or ensemble. Hearing the full orchestral version can be inspiring.

Developing an interest in the repertoire

Explore related repertoire, e.g. what else is available by that composer?

Exploring different approaches

There are several different approaches and organisations that advocate experiential musical learning, e.g. the Kodály method (see Idea 67), Dalcroze (see Ideas 60–61) and the Orff approach (see Idea 68).

Technology toolbox 39

"It is great to have a toolbox to get me started — there is so much music technology out there!"

Never before has there been so much technology that can be accessed to support our students' music education.

Notation packages

This is worth considering as it is helpful for composing pieces and technical exercise or sight-reading. You can also turn students' handwritten notation into proper printed notation.

Review the range though – they can be very expensive. Cheaper and more limited notation packages can be found for the iPad, e.g. Notion (**presonus.com**). And Musescore (**musescore.org**) is free.

Apps

Many are free and you can pay for the extended version if you like them. Apps for note naming, rhythm, theory, tuning, metronomes, sight-reading, composing and much more are available. Google 'the best music education apps' for a useful summary.

YouTube

Students can gain a lot of material from YouTube (even if of variable quality). It can also be motivational for a student to set up their own YouTube channel where they can record their performances.

Recording on student devices

You can use a student's mobile phone (or other device) to record voice memos or video (though do make sure you have the appropriate permissions). This can be used for duet parts, piano accompaniments, demonstrating correct rhythms or even making backing tracks. Microphones can be attached to improve the quality of recordings.

Ask the experts

Try ABRSM training events; also Music Mark and the Music Education EXPO run by Rhinegold.

Taking it further...

Here are some other useful ideas to explore:
- Download public domain music for free from **imslp.org**.
- Download ABRSM's Speedshifter (**abrsm. org**) to be able to slow down backing tracks and recordings for practise.
- E-Music Maestro (**e-musicmaestro. com**) has free sample aural tests.

40 Sight-reading

"With sight-reading, I find a little and often is the way to go."

Have a bank of bought and home-made resources to use with your students to develop excellent sight-reading skills from the start. Singing in a choir or playing in an ensemble also improves sight-reading.

Quick studies

Give a student a weekly easy piece(s) for quick study. Use a combination of fun, familiar pieces and music that builds the skills they lack (e.g. top register notes, tricky rhythms, unfamiliar key signature, etc.).

Rhythm and pitch flashcards

Tap or clap flashcard rhythms (pianists use both knees – for right hand rhythm and left hand rhythm). Increase the rhythm difficulty.

Place a limited number of pitch flashcards on the music stand. Ask the student to play them in that order, then change the order and ask the student to read them in the different order.

Sight-reading study guides

Have a range of sight-reading available, including exam boards' past tests. Loan them out to your students on an ongoing basis.

A line of music a day

Give the student a line of music from any appropriate material to read each day, for regular practice.

> **Top tip**
>
> Encourage students to maintain the pulse when sight-reading. In order to do this, they need to carry on playing, even if this means missing out notation. Different ways to train for this include playing with a backing track, with a keyboard drumbeat or with a metronome.

Windows

The best sight-readers tend to read a few beats or even bars ahead using their short-term memory (memorising previous bars). Training for this can include using an envelope with a window. The window is placed over a bar. The student studies it, and then moves on.

Ensemble playing material

The struggling sight-singer will gain much from singing in a choir, as will an instrumentalist playing in an orchestra, to develop the skills of looking ahead and maintaining the pulse. Piano and keyboard players can develop these skills playing in duets or trios.

Find, say and play 41

"This game is a simple but effective way to help students learn their notes."

Find, say and play is a simple game in which a student finds given notes on their instrument, says what they are and then plays them. It is a fantastic game, and can really reinforce note-reading skills as a student progresses.

Find, say and play game

To play this game, provide a random series of notes (maximum 10) on a stave and ask your student to:

● **find** the notes on their instrument (developing their muscle memory), then

● **say** what they are (so you know that they are actually identifying the individual notes rather than just reading the pattern), and then

● **play** them (reinforcing where the note is on the instrument).

Provide a different series of notes for the game each week and then get your student to showcase how well they achieve the task.

Find, say and play game extended

Try getting the student to devise their own Find, say and play games including scale or arpeggio patterns. They could write some without the lines of the stave and then try to play the pattern – recognising the spacing of the different intervals.

Taking it further...

Find, say, play games are included in *Get Set! Piano* and are also available on the *Get Set!* product pages on collins.co.uk.

Anecdote

I remember adopting students for whom every single note had previously always been written on their pieces, and having students saying things like: 'That's a one' (reading finger numbers rather than notes). Learning to read notation was something we had to spend a huge amount of time on, and this needed to be done gently to maintain their self-esteem. Playing games like Find, say and play even against the clock (if a competitive child), can make note-reading fun and build confidence.

42 Steps to improvising

"It don't mean a thing if it ain't got swing."

Students gain much from the complete freedom improvisation allows them to explore their instruments without the constraints of set notation.

Begin with rhythm

● Start with call and response using rhythm patterns – you perform a short rhythm pattern on body percussion and the student copies. Start with the pulse and then simple rhythm patterns and get progressively harder (e.g. sub-divide the beat, swing the beat, introduce triplets and rhythms in different time signatures).

● For advanced students use syncopated rhythms, rock and different Latin rhythms.

Top tip

Understanding phrasing is essential for improvising. As you play, get students to walk during the phrase then stop when it ends. Alternatively, they can use a scarf or a finger waved to draw the phrase (see Idea 35). Ensure students realise silences are essential parts of phrases.

Bonus idea

Explore jazz scales (blues) and chords (7ths, 9ths, 11ths) on a keyboard or guitar and play scales in jazz rhythms (swung).

Using pitch

● Use the same call and response idea as rhythm above, using one single pitch then moving on to additional notes, gradually extending the note range to include notes from various scales, e.g. pentascales (C major – C D E F G) or the jazz scale (C E flat F G flat G B flat C). Provide students with boxes of suggested notes.

● You could also blank out bars in a piece of music the student is playing so they can select their own notes and improvise instead.

Use notes from a current piece

● Use just a short motif from a piece or one bar of melody to build further melodies from.

Tell a story

● Very young children love telling a story by improvising on their instruments. You could use a picture to inspire this.

Encourage lots of listening

● There are lots of fantastic examples of improvising on YouTube and iTunes.

The life-size stave 43

"The life-size stave is a real hit with my students!"

A life-size stave is a multi-sensory way (see Idea 69) of teaching musical notation. Using the whole body can be an effective way of helping students to remember.

Create a stave on the floor using masking tape (see Idea 28), or alternatively find an old piece of carpet or a carpet hall runner and use black carpet tape/masking tape to mark the lines of the stave. (If you make one yourself using carpet, it is transportable and you will be able to use it everywhere you go.) For pianists, provide the grand stave (treble and bass clefs), and mark middle C with a different-coloured tape in the middle.

Explore some of these activities using your life-size stave:

◐ Sing the note names: Ask the student to sing the letter names of the different pitches as they stand in the relevant space on the stave. Say and sing the line notes and the space notes of the treble clef.

◐ Jumping notes: This is a group game – assign each student a note or number of notes; they need to jump on the stave when their note is held up.

◐ Musical twister: Randomly ask students to use their hands and feet (as in the game Twister) to put notes on the stave (or 'spell' out a word).

◐ Stand and play: Stand on the note pitch and play the corresponding note on an instrument. Use a picture of the keyboard for pianists.

Top tip

Encourage parents/carers to help their children practise note recognition by creating a life-size stave in the home.

Anecdote

I remember one student who simply didn't understand lines and spaces. To her it wasn't a space because you couldn't see through the paper. By using an actual ladder, holding steps and pushing hands through the space, she then understood the principle of lines and spaces on the stave.

44 The circle of fifths

"One of the ways I've found to get my students to practise scales is using the circle of fifths."

The circle of fifths can be useful in instrumental lessons to organise sequentially scales and arpeggios practice and also to develop key awareness in sight-reading.

Perform it

Find all the keys by following the pattern of notes: for the sharp keys, play C then move up a perfect 5th to G, etc.; for the flat keys, play C then move down a perfect 5th to F, etc. The order of the sharps and flats can also be found by moving up/down a perfect 5th (F sharp, C sharp, etc.; B flat, E flat, etc.)

Learning scales

Use the circle of fifths to structure scale learning (knowing the sharps and flats in the key) and for your students to use when practising. For example, start with C and G major scales and play the major and relative minor along with the accompanying arpeggios; when these are secure move on to D and A, then E and B, etc.

Top tip

Remember the order of sharps and flats in the circle of fifths using the rhyme:
Father **C**hristmas **G**ave **D**ad **A**n **E**lectric **B**lanket (sharps); **B**lanket **E**xplodes **A**nd **D**ad **G**ets **C**old **F**eet (flats). Or: **F**ather **C**harles **G**oes **D**own **A**nd **E**nds **B**attle (sharps); **B**attle **E**nds **A**nd **D**own **G**oes **C**harles' **F**ather (flats).

Sight-reading

Invite your student to use the circle of fifths regularly as part of their sight-reading studies to identify key signatures and modulations (using accidentals to help). Reference it before playing a sight-reading piece in the lesson and encourage the student to do this at home. There are other ways to find the key, but this is worth reinforcing.

Transposing

Take a small melodic passage (e.g. 'Happy Birthday to you') and transpose it through the circle of fifth keys with your student. This will take some time, but is a valuable way of exploring new keys.

"I find intervals tricky but simply keep working at them."

Students need a range of strategies and tools to help identify and understand intervals.

Here are some useful strategies for you to explore with your students:

Interval number

Students first need to identify the interval number – this can be done by writing note names and counting up the letters from bottom to top. Remind your students to count every letter, e.g. the interval C– F is C (1), D (2), E (3), F (4) – a fourth.

You can start exploring this straight away with your beginners. Pick one interval a week for a student to find in the music they are playing. Get them to highlight these on the music and aurally identify them too.

Type of interval

The trickier aspect of intervals is identifying what type of interval it is, e.g. perfect fourth or augmented fourth... Here are some ideas:

○ **Grid:** Produce a grid for your students to fill in (giving interval name and space for the student to write in the number of semitones) – this is more fun than a blank page.

○ **Number of semitones:** Identify intervals in a straightforward key (e.g. C for pianists; D for strings). Use this as a model. Count the number of semitones in each interval. Use this as a reference to work out interval names of notes in other keys.

○ **Scales:** Write the major scale (if known) of the lower note. Does the higher note appear in the scale? If yes, it is major or perfect. If not, work out the difference in semitones to identify it.

Top tip

Check understanding of double sharps and double flats. Be aware that these notes can commonly result in diminished and augmented intervals.

Taking it further...

My students find it really helpful if I relate intervals to transposition. I ask questions like: 'The music is in C major. If we were to transpose it up a major second what would the key be?' (Answer: D Major). This helps them understand the practical value of understanding intervals, which in most cases they find very tricky.

46 Chord grids

"I used the chord grids in my GCSE composition lesson — my teacher was very impressed!"

As students progress, a working knowledge of chords and their inversions is required for music theory and can also be useful for composing and playing by ear (especially on piano or guitar). A chord grid provides a visual representation of all these chords and the different inversion bass notes. Your students will find them really useful and easy to create and use.

Top tip

Many children don't understand Roman numerals. Make sure you teach the main symbols up to 7. Explain that you only use two symbols up to 7 – the I and V.

Top tip

Students can find it helpful to colour-code the primary/power chords – I (tonic), IV (sub-dominant) and V (dominant) – on their chord charts.

Why does this grid work well?

Students are writing the scale in sequence, which removes the margin for error. They also see chords in context (how they relate to one another).

This is how to create a chord grid (see example opposite):

● Write out the scale of the key you want to produce a chord grid, for at the top of the page.

● Label your grid with the chord numbers down the side (using Roman numerals if possible) and a, b, c (for root, first inversion and second inversion) over the top.

● Insert the first, third and fifth note of the scale across the first three boxes for chord I.

● Continue inserting the note names down each column in the sequence of the notes of the scale. Remember to put in the sharps and flats as necessary.

● Check that your chord grid is accurate – if you have a keyboard, play the chords.

Chord grid example

Scale: C major

C   D   E   F   G   A   B   C

	a	b	c
I	C	E	G
II	D	F	A
III	E	G	B
IV	F	A	C
V	G	B	D
VI	A	C	E
VII	B	D	F

Taking it further...

You can explain how the major scale can be harmonised using the three-chord trick – by just using the three chords I, IV and V.
Scale:
C D E F G A B C
Chord:
I V I IV I IV V I

Bonus idea

Axis of Awesome have produced some fun YouTube videos demonstrating how many familiar songs use the same four chords (I V vi IV). Students really enjoy these clips – but do watch them first to check for suitability of language as some are better than others in this respect!

47 Steps to a melody

"I wanted to be able to write my own songs and now I can!"

There is so much for a student to learn from writing a simple melody (notation, time signatures, keys, using Italian terms, etc.). A structured approach can provide a good starting point.

Here is a structured approach to writing a melody for you to explore with your students:

○ Set out how many bars you plan to write your melody over (4, 8, 12 and 16 bars work best).

○ Compose an appropriate rhythm – common folk tune rhythms can be used if needed: *Twinkle, twinkle* (4/4); *Lavender's blue* (3/4); *The Grand Old Duke of York* (2/4); *Hickory dickory dock* (6/8).

○ Work out whether your rhythms are in two- or four-bar phrases – at this stage, try to keep them even.

○ Decide on the key of the music and write out the scale and the chords for that key (see Idea 46).

○ Use just one chord per bar and set out a chord sequence putting cadences in at the end of the first half – either imperfect cadence (any chord to V) or interrupted (chord V to VI) – and at the end – either perfect (V – I) or plagal (IV – I). Some useful chord progressions include: I VI IV V or I VI V I.

○ Base the melody around the chord sequence: use sequences, scale and arpeggio patterns, passing notes, repeated notes and auxiliary notes. Check they fit with the harmony. Start and end on the tonic unless the melody has an anacrusis (upbeat) when the dominant note of the key works well.

○ Give the melody a title, write appropriate tempo markings, dynamics and performance directions.

Top tip

The pentatonic scale (e.g. the black notes on the piano) is a really useful tool for teaching melody-writing and improvisation. A lot of folk music melodies are based on this scale.

Bonus idea

Inform your student about the three-chord trick (see Taking it further in Idea 46) and how the major scale can be harmonised using just three chords (I, IV and V).

Quiz sheets for 48 note-reading

"My little one will fill in note quizzes for hours; it beats her sitting playing on the iPad."

Students can really benefit from doing some work on note-reading away from their instrument. Quiz sheets are fantastic for this. Here are some example note-reading quiz sheets for you to create for your students.

Identifying words from given notation

Ask students to work out a word spelt in music notation, using the letters for the note names and including R (for rest) and P (for pause) – with the pause being read before the note name, e.g.

Other useful words using this set of letters include: ACE, APE, BARGE, BEE, BEED, BEAR, BED, CAB, CABBAGE, CAFE, CAGE, DEAR, DEAF, EGG, EAR, FACE, FEAR, FEED, FREE, GEAR, PEA, READ, RED, RAG.

Writing notes for given words

Writing the notes is much trickier and students will need to be confident writing the notes on the stave in order, before attempting this (see Top tip for a strategy to check this). It is the reverse of the activity above; this time the student spells out the notes on the stave. Any of the words above work just as well for this activity.

Top tip

As noted in Idea 43, the lines and spaces of the stave can be confusing for some students. Ask your students to draw a stave themselves and number the lines from the bottom (1 to 5). Explain that the notes 'on the lines' have the line of the stave going through them, whereas the notes in the 'spaces' don't. Check their understanding by asking them to draw the notes on the lines and in the spaces.

49 Musical detective

"Music can come alive when I understand how and why the composer has written it."

Work with your student to find out the background, musical content and context of a piece of music. This can improve a student's musical understanding, aural skills and ability to interpret the music.

Look at a piece of music with your student and explore these ideas for making your student a musical detective:

● **Rhythm:** Can your student describe the rhythm and time signature? Can they clap or write any repeated rhythms from the piece?

● **Tonality and harmony:** Can your student identify the key signature and any key changes in the music? If the piece is for keyboard or an ensemble, can the student identify the harmony?

Top tip

BBC GCSE Music Bitesize and Classic FM online are both good places to suggest students go to as starting points for research.

Taking it further...

Some pieces of music have intriguing titles for students to research to encourage more meaning in their playing. For example, *Für Elise* by Beethoven translated reads 'For Elise' –students can enjoy researching who Elise was.

● **Structure:** Can your student work out the structure of the music? Encourage them to use the specific structure, e.g. A B (binary), A B A (ternary), A B A C A (rondo). Encourage them to research other forms, such as theme and variation, sonata form or fugue (if a keyboard piece).

● **Melody and pitch:** Can the student identify whether the melody moves mostly by step (conjunct) or leaps (disjunct)? Does it include any scale or arpeggio patterns, sequences or motifs? What is the range of notes used?

● **Dynamic, articulation and tempo markings:** Can the student identify all the markings on the score?

● **Texture/parts** (if relevant): How many parts are included? Identify these as soprano, alto, tenor and bass if helpful.

● **Historical background and context** (including style): Ask the student to investigate the composer and title and what period and style of music it is.

Chain walking 50

"This is my favourite way to get students to 'live' the pulse!"

Experiencing pulse and rhythm at the same time using the whole body is a very effective technique to develop the ability to maintain the pulse. Chain walking (a Kodály technique) achieves this aim.

This is how to chain walk:

○ Teach this rhyme:

Pulse   is   a   steady beat,

Feel it   moving   in your feet,

Always   steady, keep in   time,

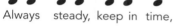

Tap your feet and say this rhyme.

○ Walk the pulse as you say the rhyme out loud.

○ Carry on walking the pulse but now clap the syllables of the rhyme (the rhythm). This can take rather a lot of practice, especially with young students.

○ Choose a different rhyme or rhythm to clap as you continue to walk the pulse.

Consolidate the rhythms by making rhythm flashcards for each of the lines of the rhyme. Encourage the students to match the notated rhythms to the lines of the rhyme.

Top tip

You can also get students to experience pulse and rhythm at the same time by sitting (cross-legged) facing a partner. One student taps the rhythm on their partner's shoulders and the other student taps the pulse on their partner's knees.

Bonus idea

Another useful rhyme for teaching pulse and rhythm is:
March together keep a beat.
Feel that movement in your feet.
Stand together in a row.
Marching forward off we go.

51 The walking scale

"By walking the scale, I properly understood the intervals between the notes."

Some students find it helpful to learn a scale using a multi-sensory approach (see Idea 69). Turning the scale into a life-size activity (learning via the whole body) can help make learning scales more memorable, fun and interactive.

This method uses steps to mark the tones and semitones, using singing then instruments to help learn the notation.

○ Explain to your student that scales are a pattern of tones and semitones. Play some examples of tones and semitones on your instrument.

○ Play your student a major scale, then sing the scale with them (to la).

○ Show students the pattern on the instrument (if is easy to see, e.g. on a piano) or use the diagram below if clearer. You can also use objects like bricks or stones carefully spaced.

C → D → E → F → G → A → B → C
tone tone semi- tone tone tone semi-
             tone   tone

○ Walk through the pattern of the major scale singing the letter names of the scale at the same time. Do a stride for a tone and a smaller step for a semitone (include leap for the tone and a half in the harmonic minor when you do that).

○ Next, walk through the pattern of the major scale with the instrument. First of all silently finger the notes on the instrument (singing the letter names) and then play the notes at the same time as stepping the pattern.

Repeat this for the harmonic minor and the melodic minor. Explain to the student that the natural minor (or Aeolian mode) is the descending scale of the melodic minor.

Bonus idea

It's a good idea to teach all students how to sing all the major, harmonic, melodic and natural minors. This aural ability will really help them when notation and fingering become challenging.

"It drives me bonkers when my students simply practise from beginning to end, so the start is brilliant and the performance gradually declines!"

Break up a piece of music into smaller sections and ask your students to practise these sections in a random order as a puzzle to make sure the 'liked' or 'easier' sections aren't just played over and over again.

To prepare this idea, break up the piece of music into small bite-sized sections. This can be done in phrases or simply four to eight bars at a time (depending on the length of the music). Label each section with a letter name (A, B, C, etc.). Use these sections to create puzzles for practice.

Puzzles

Create a range of puzzles based on the different labelled sections of the music, e.g. ask the pupil to practise sections B D F A C E one week and A F C D E B the next.

Use puzzle practice to help the student to identify which letter bars they find the most tricky so they can practise those more.

Talk to your student about how successful they have found using this approach to learning a piece of music.

Anecdote

When I borrowed some music from my teacher, I noticed it had alphabetical letters all over it. When I asked what it was for, she replied that students need to learn music in bite-sized sections, rather than having to do things all at once. The letters were simply logical sections to work on and master in time.

53 Memorising song lyrics

"The face helps tell the story, so singing from memory is vitally important."

Singing from memory helps a singer to communicate the understanding and meaning behind the words (the full story) better and give a more musical performance. This idea gives some suggestions for helping to learn the lyrics from memory.

When learning a song, it really helps to put the song in context first:

◗ Research the meaning of the song: was it from a particular time in history? Does it have any social implications?

◗ If the lyrics are in a foreign language, find a good quality translation (e.g. books such as *Lieder line by line*). Beware the English translations given in some published versions as these often will be given to make the best sense of the idea, but they are rarely anything approaching accurate on a word-for-word basis, so stresses can end up on strange words.

Here are some hints and tips to help your students memorise the words of a song:

◗ **Muddle up the lyrics:** Ask your students to write out the words one sentence at a time on small cards. They then muddle the cards up and put them into the correct order again. They should check how accurate they have been and repeat.

◗ **Facial expressions:** Encourage your students to match their facial expressions with the words.

◗ **Cartoons:** Encourage your students to draw a cartoon with key words from the song included in the cartoon. They should draw it several times and include different words each time.

◗ **Gestures:** Divide the words of the song into short phrases and write them on large pieces of card. Place them around the room. Ask your students to stop at each card, say the words but also include some acting gestures to go with them.

Top tip

Encourage students to practise improvising words in case they ever forget them. Give them a copy of the words of their song with certain lines blanked out. Encourage them to fit something appropriate in there instead.

Tips for teaching **54**
small groups

"We always work together in our lesson, so I don't need to worry about getting it wrong!"

Small group teaching can be an excellent and cost-effective introduction to an instrument. It can be very rewarding to deliver, and has the added benefit that students learn from each other.

Here are some tips for effective small group teaching:

○ Holistic teaching is essential here (using methods such as Kodály and Dalcroze, see Ideas 60–70) as you are teaching general musicianship as well as just an instrument.

○ Essentials of rhythm, rhythmic patterns, note names and movement become as much a part of the learning process as pitching – singing should be there in abundance from day one.

○ Activities need to involve the whole group for 99.9 percent of the time – even if in a different capacity – to keep all students engaged. For example, students can clap rhythms, perform ostinati, sing, dance, conduct or listen while others play.

○ Arms and hands will get tired easily at the start, so alternate playing activities with learning about rhythm, singing a song, starting to pitch, etc.

○ Learn to sing a melody, then to try to play it – without notation. Where appropriate, perhaps sing it as a round then develop to playing *and* singing rounds.

○ Try to have some form of accompaniment or backing track. It helps maintain the pulse and also gives a very clear start and finish point.

○ Always use the same introduction to pieces. After a few weeks, don't tell them which piece they are going to play or sing, just play the introduction and see if they can pick it up.

○ Use of note value flashcards (see Idea 27) and sol-fa is very helpful in early learning as it removes the need for music books and stands, which take up extra space and time.

Top tip

Always have a few small percussion instruments available (small shakers, claves, bells) that can be used if a student's instrument is out of action or forgotten.

Bonus idea

See Idea 20 for a sample lesson plan for teaching small groups.

55 Group learning techniques

"Group teaching provides a collaboratively–developmental environment in which the students learn from one another."

When teaching in groups it is important to find ways to keep all your students engaged and appropriately challenged. The techniques in this idea can be used with groups of every size.

○ **Start with a song:** Once instruments are ready, sing a song. If possible, sing a round.

○ **Learn to play songs:** Take a song and learn to play it, then develop this into singing and playing a round in alternation (e.g. perform *Frère Jacques* as a four-part round in which each group sings the song then plays it then sings it again – it makes for a good length of piece which retains its interest).

○ **Develop scales:** Scales are useful for learning patterns, but don't try to use all the notes straight away:

▸ Use note value flashcards (see Idea 27) and select a simple four-beat rhythm (e.g. *crotchet, two quavers, crochet, crotchet*) to play on each note. Choose a different rhythm pattern each lesson.

▸ With a 'high flyer' student, let them try playing an octave higher, or in thirds or sixths to give them variety and make them think.

▸ If possible, have a keyboard/piano harmonisation to accompany scales and a standard two-bar introduction.

○ **Learning pieces:** Use the 'sound before symbol' method (see Idea 3) as much as possible in the group situation as it is a much quicker way to learn and, because the learning is usually more holistic in group teaching, there will be plenty of repetition for the note-reading to sink in.

○ **Revise previously-learnt pieces:** Go back to previously-learnt pieces, so that there is always one piece that is played totally fluently every lesson.

Top tip

When teaching a group, there is a stronger requirement for repetition of activities. This gives pleasure to the group because they can all partake and achieve. By repeating ideas in a way that extends and develops them, you will keep the ideas interesting for all learners.

Taking it further...

Group playing can result in a really big corporate sound. This, with encouragement, means all students will start to play even the simplest melody with a lovely rich tone.

Whole class ensemble teaching

"Our whole class instrumental lessons are the children's highlight of the week!"

This idea provides a simple outline for a whole class lesson for you to adapt to your needs.

Warm-up activity

Start the lesson with a warm-up activity – make this physical if possible, e.g. walking around the room to music as crotchets, minims, quavers (see Idea 60).

Revise the class rules

These can be devised together as a group and then written out for each student or kept in a folder or book to use throughout the course. Get different students to read a rule and say together a class motto.

Revise notes learnt or previous material

Students will need to be reminded where they got to last lesson. They get a great deal from repetition and feel safe doing things they can already do.

Introduce a new piece – but sing and clap it first

Preparation can include: learning the rhythms in the music from flashcards; singing the melody before playing it; saying the rhythm and note names before playing them. Demonstrate on your instrument so children have a visual prompt too.

Improvisation and performance activities

Include some creative improvisation and performance activities for solos, group and whole class.

Learning harvest and finishing activity

Record on the board from the students what they have learnt, and from this assess what they've missed. Have a regular activity to end the lesson.

Top tip

In a whole class situation, backing tracks can be a lifesaver. They give a good pulse to follow and make things sound (in the learning stages) more attractive to the ear! Make sure they are not too fast.

57 Running an ensemble

"Playing an instrument as a group really boosts the students' confidence and self-esteem."

A room full of 35 children and instruments can be a daunting prospect, but with attention to details of organisation, student management and regular work patterns, it can soon become a very pleasant music-making environment.

Organisation strategies

Think about your organisation strategies well before the first session. Consider the following:

○ Sitting/standing: Consider the length of the session. If it is only 30 minutes it's probably easier/quicker for standing players to remain standing. Any longer and they will need to be able to sit.

○ Music stands: If using music stands, try to have these out ready.

○ Instrument cases: Are students to get instruments out of cases and then come into your 'circle' or do they keep cases/instruments together? This will depend on the instrument. With smaller instruments, keeping cases with the instrument enables the student to rest the instrument on the case when doing other activities. It is also easier when they are first learning to assemble the instrument.

○ Setting up and tuning: Setting up and tuning can take a long time so, if possible, have the instruments ready before the students arrive. If not, encourage helpers to assist and ask the students to have their instruments prepared (handing to you) for tuning quickly.

○ Signals: Control of noise can be a challenge so you need to have a signal that *always* means silence (e.g. holding the bow/instrument in the air). Most instrumentalists should develop a good 'rest position'.

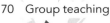

- **Establishing a routine:** Follow the same patterns every lesson until the routine is established, then you can relax a bit.

- **Managing resources:** If handing out books/music, *always* use the same system (e.g. pass a section's music to their 'leader' for them to distribute). Collect at the end of the lesson in the same way.

Student management strategies

- **School behaviour management policy:** If running your ensemble within a school, check the school behaviour management policy and mirror it. Be consistent – always doing what you are saying you are going to do. If you encounter any behaviour issues, always give a warning first.

- **Set clear expectations:** Devise a set of rules with the group and revisit them when occasion dictates. Have clear consequences if the rules are broken and always follow through.

- **Maximise understanding:** Use as many ways as possible to maximise possible understanding – speaking, demonstrating, drawing things and providing handouts for the children to write on. Behaviour issues usually only arise when students are bored, don't understand or aren't properly occupied.

- **Give praise:** Talk positively and regularly praise students for doing the right thing.

- **Giving instructions:** Make instructions clear and short.

Top tip

It is really helpful if you find it difficult to learn names, if the students wear name labels. They can make these themselves, but it's incredibly useful to you when giving instructions, praise and discipline.

Taking it further...

It is helpful to set up the room consistently each session, with students in the same position (unless you decide to change it) and with instruments/cases/music stands consistently placed. Extra pairs of hands, either from a class teacher or teaching assistant, or a willing parent, can be a huge help – let them learn the instrument too.

Bonus idea

Encourage older, more mature students to take on the role of helpers – give them a badge to wear as a reward.

58 Instruments and accessories

"Having instruments correctly set up, although initially more expensive, can save time and money in the long run."

It is worth spending a little time at the start to get the right instruments and make sure they are in good working order with all the required accessories before you start a series of group lessons.

Here are some hints and tips for managing your instruments for group teaching.

○ Choosing instruments: In group situations you need to have sturdy, well-constructed instruments with good accessories (these won't be the cheapest) in order that you can spend time teaching rather than repairing/adjusting each lesson.

Top tip

Have a small toolkit suitable for your instrument, so that you can make simple alterations quickly and easily yourself. If you don't have any other adult support, ask one of the more mature/older students to be in charge while you sort an instrument out.

Taking it further...

Make friends with your local specialist instrument repairer. They will often do a quick repair if you use them regularly.

○ Strings: String instruments will benefit from having some decent strings fitted if at all possible.

○ Cases: Ensure cases work properly so that instruments can be taken out without damage.

○ Accessories: Make sure that 'extras' such as bow rosin, valve oil, reeds, cleaning cloths, etc. are all readily available so that you can get on with the business of teaching.

○ Chairs: Players who need to sit to play, need comfortable chairs at the correct height, so that they develop good posture from the beginning. Try wood blocks under the back legs (or 'leg-ups') to improve the seat angle so that students can sit with their feet on the floor but comfortably.

○ Music stands: If needed, these should be quick and easy to adjust and very stable, to avoid accidents and/or time-wasting while adjusting them.

○ Extra pair of hands: An extra pair of hands (or two) to help set up big groups, is invaluable.

Finding the right material for groups

"There is so much music available that I just don't know where to start!"

Finding the right resources for group teaching and ensembles can take a little time. The best approach is to buy a selection of resources to dip into and create your own as well, so that you can build up a bank of exactly what you need. This idea gives a few pointers to help get you started.

Explore the following:

● **Mixed instrument resources:** If you have mixed instruments in your group, you will need to do some research to find music books that cover all your instruments with pieces that match on a page-for-page basis – some cello and violin books, for example, don't do this despite being part of the same series.

● **Online resources:** Look for online resources – there are lots around. Some firms supply complete packages which work with a classroom whiteboard, show the notes being played and are a good back-up package to get you going.

● **Singing resources:** Starting with rounds and rhymes and singing before you play means that the need for instrumental ensemble music is put off for a little while. You will need to find some good singing resources with simple rounds and rhymes (see Idea 32).

● **Early ensemble music:** Early ensemble music (e.g. *Stringsets*, *Kaleidoscope* and ABRSM/Trinity materials) can work very well for group lessons.

● **Photocopying:** Some group tuition music books now allow you to make a limited number of photocopies of certain pages. Always check and make sure you abide by photocopying law.

● **Create your own:** If you're going to make your own arrangements for your group, do it on a computer programme so that you can find it again in the future and change key or clef easily for a different combination of instruments.

> **Top tip**
>
> BBC *Ten Pieces* provides a whole range of simplified free orchestral arrangements of the classical pieces included in the repertoirs from Grade 1 to 3; just search online for 'BBC Ten Pieces'.

60 Introduction to Dalcroze Eurhythmics

"Being introduced to Dalcroze has invigorated the way I teach and changed the way I hear, read, process, and perform music."

Dalcroze Eurhythmics teaches and gives experience of music through the use of movement in three distinct areas which integrate into the whole: rhythmics; ear training and improvisation.

In instrumental lessons it is all too easy to concentrate on the instrument and technique and lose sight of the music. Use some simple Dalcroze-style movement activities to help develop musicianship skills.

Improvisation march

Ask your students to march around the room while you improvise some music to march to. As confidence increases, start to introduce very small, subtle changes: major/minor; forte/piano; high/low pitch. What effect does this have on the movement? Encourage the students to exaggerate the emotion of the musical movement.

Dalcroze flashcards

Ask students to move in response to you improvising a simple rhythm that uses only crotchets and quavers. Introduce the Dalcroze flashcards (see below) and ask students to identify which flashcard fits which movement. Keep it simple and don't introduce new cards until the first ones are secure. Always remember, sound before symbol.

Move then 'write'

Play a one- or two-bar simple phrase (just crotchets and quavers to start with) and ask your student to echo the rhythm pattern in steps. Repeat a few more times until it is secure, then ask them to 'write' the rhythm using the Dalcroze flashcards. When each note value is secure, add a new note value (e.g. minim or semiquaver). Always step the notes before attempting to 'write' them.

Dalcroze flashcards

 walk

 jogging

 stride

 running faster

 skip-ty

More Dalcroze Eurhythmics

"Can we play games again today?"

One of the biggest joys in my teaching has been that all children relish ball games. It's not just that they enjoy it so much, but because they learn so much without realising it. It can be months, even years, down the line when all the connections suddenly 'ping' together.

Here are some Dalcroze activities that my students love:

Ball-bouncing

A really enjoyable activity for youngsters is to bounce a ball on the first beat of the bar – this builds up a strong feeling of the importance of the first beat. Very gradually introduce changes of time signature and don't be afraid of trying 5/4 or 7/4. Students develop the following skills:

❍ the ability to listen and react

❍ the feeling of the different time signatures through the physical gesture

❍ a sense of rebound in the body.

Feeling phrasing

Play a fairly simple piece of music (e.g. Handel's *Rigaudon in G*) and encourage your student(s) to listen for the structure – drawing the shape and length of the phrases in the air. At the early stages don't be too concerned about 'getting it right'. Whilst there are some responses that may be considered 'wrong', the joy of music is that we all hear it differently and, while some may consider it an eight-bar phrase, others might prefer to think of it as two four-bar phrases. The importance, at the beginning, is to build up the *feeling* of where and how phrases move through space and how that helps the natural shape of them. Using a floaty scarf can give even more sense of shape and style to the progressive movement.

Top tip

Build a collection of Dalcroze accessories: balls (bigger ones are much easier for small hands to catch), very light scarves that can 'float' through the air, shakers with differing sounds, claves, etc.

Taking it further...

These suggestions are only the tip of the iceberg; try to go on a Dalcroze course for teachers (**www.dalcroze.org.uk**).

62 Everyday aural training

"Once we started doing a little every lesson it all became familiar and seemed much easier!"

Developing hearing and listening skills feeds the whole musician and should be an essential component of all music lessons. In my work with young children I always insist that I teach music not 'the piano' or 'the violin'.

Here are some simple ideas for developing aural training regularly in your lessons:

● Take any piece of music and think of the aural possibilities. From an early age, ask students to listen for phrase shapes and style, e.g. how long is each phrase?

● Develop the ideas of structure from these simple, short early phrases to give a start to an awareness of form from the very beginning.

● Don't worry about using 'proper' terms, a simple 'A' or 'B' section description is quite clear.

> **Top tip**
>
> Every musical activity that we undertake contains many aural elements that we don't notice. As teachers we need to look at identifying and utilising aural awareness in all the music we do, e.g. in listening, memorising, pitching, rhythmic perception and harmony, to name but a few. Developing aural awareness is about far more than passing the aural section of an exam.

● Sing as a matter of course! Singing is a skill for all musicians, but not all learners have singing confidence. If a young singer always sings back at too low a pitch, play them a lower pitched tune to sing back – it's not that they *can't* but that they haven't learnt how to change the pitch of their voice. Start with the area they can pitch (it may be only two or three notes) and then gradually expand outwards.

● Encourage 'sing as you play' if possible (not wind players or singers!) so that it is introduced from the very beginning.

● Develop feelings of pulse and rhythm from the beginning; just keep it simple to start with (e.g. only crotchets and quavers).

● Play the game 'SWAP': you clap crotchets and the student claps quavers. Then shout SWAP and change parts. Make variations to the rhythm patterns, but don't introduce a new note (e.g. minim or semiquaver) until you are sure students have grasped the crotchet and quavers.

Aural training –
easy harmony

"I always feared doing aural tests, but now we do fun games instead of tests!"

Introducing an awareness of harmony does not have to wait until students have to listen for it in their Grade 6 aural tests. Introduce the concept early and through the music they are learning. Understanding harmony and musical structure will enhance students' performance skills and make aural tests a breeze!

Becoming aware of the harmony of accompaniments and musical structure will improve the sense of style and phrasing in their playing.

○ From an early age, ask students to listen out for harmony (but don't initially use that word, just 'listen for' is sufficient, e.g. 'listen for a surprise in the music').

○ The fact that cadences aren't introduced until Grade 6 aural tests does *not* mean that they shouldn't be introduced earlier. Start by listening for a simple, perfect cadence – heard at the end of so many early grade pieces. Identify and name it to begin the idea of hearing harmony.

○ Play the Cadence game.

Cadence game

○ Start by using only perfect and interrupted cadences.

○ Make up a simple tune. As you play, the student decides whether the music is going to surprise and carry on (interrupted cadence) or finish (perfect cadence). Students usually love the 'naughty' interrupted cadence. The student directs, using different movements, how they want the music to move – you may end up with a very short (or long!) piece.

○ As your students' playing skills develop, try swapping parts – the student makes up the tune and you direct the cadences.

○ When the students are confident with perfect and interrupted cadences, bring in the imperfect cadence, and later on the plagal cadence.

Top tip

Encourage students to listen for harmony in their favourite songs: many 'pop' songs have a very strong I–IV–V bassline.

64 Using the Suzuki method

"The potential of every child is unlimited." Dr. Schinichi Suzuki

The Suzuki method was originally designed to follow the development of how a child learns language – by copying rather than by reading. It was first developed for young violinists but has since expanded to include viola, cello, flute, recorder and piano.

For many, learning by copying is a very easy way to learn. Students gain confidence in their ability because they feel secure about what they are doing.

● Copy games: Try including some simple copy games in every lesson – straightforward echoes can develop to call and response/ question and answer.

● Hear then play then expand: First let the students hear the music (CD, MP3, live), then learn to play what they hear. Then encourage them to keep expanding the theme they have heard, e.g. making up variations.

● Keep playing pieces you've learnt: Keep pieces in the students' repertoire for longer, so they can enjoy playing what they have learnt and knowing that they can play it – it will go on getting better and enhancing their enjoyment.

● Learning a piece by ear: Try asking your student to learn one of your 'usual' pieces just by your student copying you – does it make any difference to their playing?

● Reading music: Don't be tempted to think that Suzuki is only about playing by ear – the development of the hearing/playing is quickly followed with music reading.

Top tip

Perhaps the best known 'Suzuki tune' is *Twinkle, twinkle little star*, but that is only a starting point and should go on developing for years. Try making your own variations.

Taking it further...

Find out more at **www.britishsuzuki. org.uk.**

"I see my students taking the singing games from our lesson and teaching them to friends on the playground!"

Using singing within instrumental lessons can be very valuable for developing students' ability to internalise music (creating an inner voice) and exploring a whole host of other musical ingredients from pulse and pitch to dynamics and tempo.

Here are some simple ideas for including singing in your instrumental lessons:

○ **Sing hello:** Sing hello to a younger student at the beginning of the lesson (using a minor 3rd), e.g. 'Hello Adam'. And invite them to sing back, e.g. 'Hello Mrs Marshall'. Students gain confidence hearing their solo singing voice.

○ **Introducing a new piece:** Listen to a new piece of music without the notation and sing the melody line with your students, in short phrases. Encourage the student to follow the shape of the musical line with their finger in the air. Then introduce the notation: ask your student to follow the music score with their finger whilst singing (see Idea 24).

○ **Lyrics:** If a piece of music the student is learning has words, always sing or rap them. This will help to identify the rhythm of the music as well as the pitch.

○ **Piano-teaching:** If playing a piano, invite the student to play the bass line and sing the treble line.

○ **Understanding metre:** Use familiar rhymes to help develop awareness of different metres, e.g. *Hickory, dickory, dock* (6/8); *The Grand Old Duke of York* (2/4), etc.

○ **Singing games:** These can be a fun addition to any lesson and are an excellent way to develop your students' understanding of pitch and rhythm. There are loads of examples online, e.g. search for *Hi lo chicka lo* or *Bounce high, bounce low*.

Taking it further...

Encourage your students to join a choir, if possible. Singing in a choir develops a range of skills beneficial to instrumental learning, including improved melodic memory (useful in exam aural tests), ability to sight-sing (which can improve note-reading accuracy on an instrument) and listening skills.

66 Playing by ear

"It's music without the dots, a refreshing change."

Playing by ear is a skill which provides freedom to focus on expression and can build the self-esteem of students struggling to read music.

Students can learn to play by ear through practice and a systematic approach.

○ **Higher and lower pitches:** In the early stages students need to simply recognise higher and lower pitches. Encourage them to sing and feel the difference in their vocal chords when the pitch rises and falls, perhaps marking the higher and lower pitch with a hand motion.

○ **Identifying different intervals aurally:** Can students identify different intervals aurally and are they able to find them on their instrument? Familiar songs can help here, e.g. *Happy Birthday* starts with a repeated note then moves to the second, *Kum ba yah* starts with a third, *Away in a Manger* a fourth and *Twinkle Twinkle* a fifth. Use material students find very familiar, something they are currently studying or singing; pop favourites are excellent.

○ **An interval a week:** Choose an interval a week. Ask students to find the interval in a piece they are practising. Encourage them to sing it, and mark it on the music.

○ **Spotting sequences in music:** This is excellent training for playing by ear. There are so many sequences in music but to repeat them, a student needs to recognise them.

○ **Playing simple melodies by ear:** Once students are confident with intervals and spotting sequences, encourage them to try to play simple melodies by ear. Use very simple tunes, e.g. *Hot Cross Buns*, *Twinkle Twinkle*, *Happy Birthday*, *Frère Jacques*, *London's burning*, *Three Blind Mice*, *God Save the Queen*.

Taking it further...

For piano students, a popular piece to play by ear is *Heart and Soul* by Hoagy Carmichael. Encourage your student to listen to the original recording on YouTube.

Bonus idea !

Teach piano students the three-chord trick (see Taking it further, Idea 46).

Using the Kodály method

"Music is for everyone." Zoltan Kodály

The Kodály method is a tried and tested approach that (if taught well) can result in students building excellent musicianship. Understanding the approach and the materials available enables you to bring Kodály teaching strategies to your students.

In the 1940s, Kodály's students and colleagues began to develop a methodology based on Kodály's philosophy about music. Drawing on the best music education practice internationally, including John Curwen's sol-fa system and the rhythm names of the French movement Galin-Paris-Chevé, a methodology was born. The method primarily used the voice and the musical heritage of the country the practitioner was working in.

The approach

Kodály focused on three stages of learning: preparation, presentation, practice.

◉ Preparation: Each concept of learning is prepared (put into the subconscious): for example, marking where a rest appears in a piece of music (using 'sh' with a finger on the lips, stamping or an open-hand gesture), but not identifying it as a rest.

◉ Presentation: The student is presented with the musical concept. The student is told that where they marked the 'sh', a rest was present. They are then shown the rhythmic symbol for a rest.

◉ Practice: Finally, the student practises musical rests but in different contexts. They could clap rhythm cards with rests in, aurally identify rests when listening to a new piece of music, improvise rhythms and include rests, etc.

Top tip

Present material systematically (the easy before the difficult). Use games, puppets, flashcards and other props.

Taking it further...

Access a Kodály training course. Contact the British Kodály Academy (**britishkodaly academy.org**).

Bonus idea

These are my students' favourite Kodály melodies: *See-saw, Cobbler Cobbler, Mrs White, Apple Tree, Cuckoo, Hi lo chicka lo, Once a Man Fell in a Well, Bells in the Steeple, Teddy Bear*. These are all available online.

68 Using the Orff approach

"Young children love to move!"

The Orff approach (pioneered by the composer Carl Orff) – also known as Orff-Schulwerk – includes some useful ideas that instrumental teachers can use in their teaching, especially in small group lessons. The focus of the approach is the combining of music, language and dance.

Anecdote 💬

I recently attended an Orff UK summer school and found it a wonderful way to explore music in lots of different ways. I have used many of the rhymes, melodies and music from the course. One of my favourites is *The Alleycat* by Bent Fabric, a song about different parts of the body using the melody *Skip to my Lou* by Shirley Salmon and a dance using the *Hornpipe* tune.

Bonus idea ❗

To properly explore the method, attend a training course run by the Orff Society – who provide training across the world (**orff.org.uk**).

Here are some simple steps for exploring music with your students, influenced by an Orff approach:

○ **Listen:** Ask students to listen to a piece of music with their eyes closed and then describe what they hear.

○ **Respond with movement:** Listen again, but this time ask your students to move to the music; this could be with hand gestures or even finger gestures, dancing to the music either in a structured or unstructured way.

○ **Word rhythms chanted:** Can your students chant the words of the song, or make up word rhythms that go with the music?

○ **Word rhythms on body percussion:** Encourage students to take a rhythm from the music and perform it as body percussion on their bodies.

○ **Play by ear:** Encourage students to have a go at performing the music by ear on their instrument.

○ **Improvise/compose:** Encourage students to improvise ideas inspired by the piece (changing the music); in a group lesson, students could work with other members of the group to play in parts.

○ **Perform:** Suggest students prepare a performance of their composed piece, perhaps even with some actions included or some props.

Multi-sensory teaching

"Multi–sensory music teaching is just what it says: using all the senses to teach and learn music."

The late Margaret Hubicki (Emeritus Professor at the Royal Academy of Music) advocated teaching in a multi-sensory way for all students but especially those with a specific learning difficulty. She advised focusing on three questions with a student: What do you see? What do you feel? What do you hear?

The main senses employed in multi-sensory music teaching are sight, hearing and touch (doing). Here are some practical ideas for a multi-sensory approach in your instrumental lessons:

❍ Teaching notation: Use a life-size stave to identify the pitch with the whole body (see Idea 43).

❍ Teaching a scale: On woodwind, brass or string instruments let the student feel the fingering on the keys/holes/valves/strings whilst you play the scale, so they are hearing the notes produced and seeing the notation, but focusing on their fingering. On a keyboard, notice and feel the pattern on the keyboard whilst hearing and seeing the notation (see Idea 70).

❍ Teaching rhythm: Use Dalcroze note value names and encourage students to move as the music plays: **walk** (crotchet), **stride** (minims), **jogging** (quavers), **running faster** (four semi-quavers), **moon-walk** (semi-breve). (See Idea 60).

❍ Teaching pitch: Encourage your student (with your support) to sing the pitch names of the notes they are going to play, but also to trace their finger over the notation at the same time (feeling the shape of the melody on the page at the same time as singing it).

Top tip

Multi- sensory teaching can be seen in some of the most respected methodologies of music teaching, including those of Dalcroze, Suzuki, Kodály and Orff (see Ideas 60, 64, 67 and 68).

Anecdote

I remember a student teacher asking me what she could do to help her student learn to read music as nothing was working. I explained about multi-sensory teaching and using a life-size stave (see Idea 43). I received an excited e-mail saying the student appeared to learn more in one lesson than they had in a whole year, purely from doing.

70 Multi-sensory scales

"Scales make sense to me now — I understand the patterns and can remember them much better!"

This idea gives an example of how to use multi-sensory music teaching to teach scales to your students in a way that really works!

This idea uses the scale of C major but can easily be applied to other scales.

Hearing

● Sing to 'la' the C major scale with the student.

● Sing the ascending scale for the student to listen to, using the letter names C D E F G A B C. Then, sing the scale descending while the student follows the progress on the keyboard (or fingering on another instrument).

● For keyboard players: sing the scale to the student but this time the student fingers 1 2 3 1 2 3 4 5, etc. on a table top or closed lid as you sing up and down.

● Play the intervals of a tone and a semitone. Help the student to identify these intervals aurally within the scale.

Seeing

● Provide the student with a picture of the keyboard, fingerboard, wind instrument holes or valves showing the finger numbers for each note of the scale.

● Show the scale written out on the stave.

● If possible, show all students a keyboard to see the shape of the scale in relation to the white and black notes.

Feeling/doing

● Ask students to close their eyes and *feel* the fingering of the scale.

● Ask students to walk the pattern of the tones and semitones on the floor with large and small steps.

● Ask students to choreograph the fingering on the instrument without sound.

Top tip

Finger numbers need to be learnt. These can be reinforced with simple number songs (e.g. *One, two, three, four, five*) with finger gestures. Remember that different finger numbers are used on different instruments, e.g. first finger on the violin is second finger on the piano.

Taking it further...

For scales with sharps and flats, there can be quirky ways of remembering which sharps and flats to use, e.g. D major sharps – **F**ish and **C**hips.

Repertoire

"When I like the piece, I practise hard. If I don't like the piece, I don't practise!"

Selecting exciting and interesting repertoire for your students can give an instant boost to their practice and preparation.

To help find out what your students like, start by asking whether they prefer:

- fast or slow?
- happy or sad?
- loud or soft?
- aggressive or gentle?
- telling a story or dreaming?

Expand this range as you start to understand their preferred choices.

● **Topics and interests:** Enquire about your student's interests – not forgetting that children change their allegiances frequently – and try to find pieces to match these ideas. Giving a delightful balletic waltz when they prefer dinosaurs is a guaranteed flop.

● **Explore non-examination repertoire:** Examination repertoire is fine for examinations, but there is a vast amount of interesting music (and technical exercises) that never appears in an exam syllabus. Explore, explore, explore!

● **Student choice:** Encourage your students to search on the Internet for music that they like – even if they choose something that is far too hard, it gives a really good pointer to their choice of styles.

● **Titles:** Choose pieces with brilliant titles rather than study! One of the hardest aspects to develop can be technique if studies are seen as boring. Evocative titles can help to develop the right atmosphere and sound without your students realising… Just remember to go back and enquire *why* they played a certain way and *how* they created the sound.

● **Duets:** Finding suitable (not too hard, so that they can be learnt quickly and easily) duets to play with you and/or friends gives opportunities for students to develop their fluency as well as enjoy a performance.

Taking it further...

New music is being produced at an amazing rate. Keep exploring for new ideas by browsing in music shops, events like Rhinegold's Music Education EXPO and online.

72 Performance

"To achieve great things, two things are needed: a plan, and not quite enough time." Leonard Bernstein

Performing can give an enormous amount of pleasure to the listener, resulting in praise for the performer which, in turn, gives a great feeling of achievement and satisfaction to the performer. Knowing that you are working towards a finite point is a great motivator.

Here are some ideas for developing your students into confident performers:

❍ Performance time: Build confidence by making a 'performance time' early on in a student's learning. This can be a couple of minutes during or at the end of a lesson when the student 'performs' something.

❍ Performance etiquette: Teach performance etiquette from the very beginning. At a young student's first performance (which may only be eight bars long), they should learn to acknowledge praise by smiling and bowing – even if the performance is only to parents/carers and grandparents. Confidence will come when they have a sure sense of knowing what they are doing!

❍ Performing in different situations: Encourage performing in different situations as your students develop: small groups in the normal studio can expand to larger groups in a local hall or church (check out the piano). Working up to these performances will almost certainly motivate students to increase their level of practice.

❍ Create and perform afternoon: Occasionally set up a performance afternoon in which players of all standards join together in small groups to prepare a performance in an hour. Either give paints and paper or a picture card and ask them to prepare a performance of a picture. Remind them that there is no 'wrong' response so therefore everything will be worthy of praise.

Top tip

Occasionally a student will be very shy and nervous about performing. Ensure the selected repertoire is relatively easy for them to perform so they are most likely to succeed – then they will slowly build up belief in themselves.

Taking it further...

Explore performance opportunities in your area: local music festivals, school concerts, going to play in the local residential home, etc. This can give students a very good feeling of worth and it will motivate them to do even more.

Creating self-motivated learners

"I really, really want to be a musician, but it's so hard!"

The initial burst of enthusiasm for learning an instrument is usually very strong. The challenge is to sustain this through the trickier patches. Careful observation of what enthuses each student will give you an idea for which direction may be most successful, and will help develop students' self-motivation.

○ **Teacher's praise:** Remember that their teacher's praise is sometimes the simple reward they seek! When you praise them, they will often practise more!

○ **Rewards:** Have a large variety of rewards available – it doesn't have to be chocolate! (see Idea 75). For many students a reward of playing can be really good – either their favourite piece, or a duet with your – and it can give them back a sense of flow when they have perhaps got too bogged down in the nitty-gritty of practice.

○ **Choice of repertoire:** Wanting to learn a piece of music equates with choosing appropriate and interesting repertoire through knowledge of the student's favourite styles (see Idea 72).

○ **A reason to practise:** Never give technical work to practise just for the sake of it. Always show students how it is going to help them improve their performance so they will 'own' the idea.

○ **Practice diary:** Encourage students to keep their own practice diary so that they record what works (and doesn't work) for them. That way they can see – in print – how much they have achieved and you may, more easily, be able to identify ways to assist them.

Top tip

Development is never a smooth graph – life gets in the way... so be realistic.

Anecdote 💬

For many, old-fashioned bribes can still be the greatest motivator. I remember bribing myself to learn my Grade 8 arpeggios (which were seriously behind everything else). The Maltesers were lined up on the music stand and I was only allowed one when an arpeggio was perfect – it worked!

74 Not too much, not too hard

"People can give up before they've started if the mountain is perceived as too high to climb."

Knowing how much material to set students and how challenging it should be comes with experience. You don't want your students getting demotivated. This idea gives a few pointers to help you get started.

Top tip

If a student is really struggling with a piece, don't continue with it for too long. Instead, put it on hold, do something different and revisit it. Success at a later date can teach an important lesson: that they have improved and can now tackle something that appeared impossible.

Bonus idea

Have a full range of material for sidewards progression that simply consolidates skills. Tutor books and examination grade books rarely have enough material to cover all eventualities.

Ask the student

Students are more likely to practise something if they feel they have been included in the decision-making process. Ask for their input on choice of repertoire as well as quantity.

A balanced approach

Children can underestimate what they can achieve and may avoid more challenging material. Provide material they feel confident with but also the occasional challenge, albeit in bite-sized chunks. Give the student lots of praise for trying and reassurance that you believe they can achieve it.

An open and honest learning environment

You want your student to be able to be open and honest with you, and let you know if the material you've set is too hard, or there simply was too much to do. Ask for feedback and check body language. If a student is finding something hard or doesn't appear to understand something, then say: 'It's okay if you don't like it, we can do something else.' Or: 'Lots of people find that difficult, do you?'

"I love getting prizes from my teacher's prize bag. I work hard so I will be able to get one."

Students respond well to getting rewards for music practice and working hard towards specific goals. There are some inexpensive ways to mark achievement that can mean a great deal to a student, such as stickers, stamps and stars. This idea suggests ways to use these inexpensive rewards creatively.

Personalised stickers and stamps

Students love stickers and stamps but getting personalised ones can make those stickers more valuable to the student. There are various providers on the internet who will print stickers and produce stamps at a reasonable price that can include names or personalised messages. Use these stickers and stamps in practice books or on the music itself.

Stars

Invite your student to come up with a reward system using stars. Perhaps they want stars when they've tackled a tricky section, or star rewards out of five on performances.

Reward card

Make a reward card for your students. Every time they do good work, they get a sticker or stamp on their reward card. When they achieve a certain number of stamps or stickers, they get a reward, e.g. ten stamps to receive a prize from a prize box. This is a really effective way to motivate a student to work over a longer period of time. Prizes can be collected throughout the year whenever bargains can be picked up. Stationery and chocolate (as long as the parent is happy and there are no allergies) always appeal.

Pin badges and customised items

Various are available online, from pin badges saying 'merit' or 'well done' to custom-made items, including a whole array of materials, e.g. pens, pencils and fridge magnets. Students love this extra bit of effort.

Top tip

Having a file of motivational pieces that you are able to loan out when motivation is running low, can be just what a student needs to get them practising again. Classic favourites such as *The Entertainer* and *Für Elise;* topical theme tunes such as *Star Wars* or TV programs like *Dr Who* are good ones to start with…

76 Practice buddies

"This is a gem of an idea to help students become confident practising on their own."

Individual practice can be a struggle for students for all kinds of reasons. Creating support for when they are doing it can result in more success. Practice buddies can be anything your student needs to support their individual practice!

Here are some example practice buddies – or invent your own!

○ The mobile teacher: Use a mobile phone to record practice tasks and encouragement that the student can listen to afterwards when practising at home.

○ The playmate: Provide a backing track for your student to play along with.

○ The Facebook group: Set up a closed Facebook group where students can report to the group on practice they have completed and motivate each other. Some may wish to put their performances on their Instagram account.

○ The checklist buddy: Create a sheet for students to complete:

	Tick when completed
Warm-up long notes, exercise or scales (use the keys the pieces are written in)	
Play a piece through once to find the tricky bars	
Focus on the tricky bars Practise tricky bars in different ways (dynamics, articulation, rhythms)	
Play a favourite piece	
Improvise (even just a few notes)	
Think of three things you've achieved	

Top tip

Find good YouTube recordings of the pieces a student is playing. This can be inspiring but also very helpful for developing the aural senses (hearing what they need to play).

Building confidence and 77 self-esteem

"My teacher always has something lovely to say!"

Building our students' confidence and self-esteem will help them in all performance situations and in life in general. We build their confidence by helping them to prepare and practise so they feel confident in their playing. We build their self-esteem through our praise.

Here are some top tips for helping build confidence and self-esteem:

○ **Praise:** Every lesson, find something to praise, however small.

○ **Keep results in perspective:** Keep exam/competition results in perspective so that the 'I got more than you' syndrome doesn't become damaging.

○ **Positive outcome performances:** Arrange performances that will have a positive outcome, e.g. mini-concerts in which students give feedback to each other. These can be hugely beneficial, but encourage and expect good feedback.

○ **Dry run:** If an important concert or exam is coming up, arrange a 'dry run' beforehand to a friendly audience, e.g. a local care home.

○ **Make a recording:** Making a recording of a performance can be a useful tool, but it needs to be handled in a sensitive manner by all concerned. Often it is more important to remember the effect of the moment in terms of style and satisfaction.

○ **Performance is not the same as practice:** Many students who develop a really good practice technique sometimes forget that the criticisms they use for practice need to be put to one side in performance or they can feel nothing is ever good enough.

○ **Be constructive:** Remember to give good praise when it is due, but saying everything is excellent all the time negates the benefit.

○ **Be positive:** Develop your positive adjectives vocabulary!

Top tip

When asking students to give each other positive feedback, try asking them to use the approach of 'one good thing and one thing that could be better'. Ensure that *all* students get the opportunity to offer feedback as it helps to develop their critical thinking.

78 Music exams

"I find exams scary but exciting at the same time!"

Graded exams can be a useful guide to a student's level and allow progression to be shown, but there should be no compulsion to take them. If your students do wish to take exams, here are some top tips for being prepared.

○ **Research the exam boards' requirements:** Exams usually require a combination of pieces (selected from a choice of repertoire) and technical elements. Some exam boards also include elements such as aural, theory, sight-reading, musical knowledge and understanding, etc.

○ **Prepare all sections:** Nearly all students want to achieve good marks, yet many do not grasp the fact that ensuring that *all* sections are thoroughly known and learnt, is the easiest way to gain high marks. Study the syllabus requirements carefully and ensure all aspects are covered.

○ **Technical aspects:** Encourage the students to perform the technical aspects such as scales and studies musically. Hearing a beautifully-shaped and phrased series of scales is a rare joy.

○ **Accompanist:** If the instrument/voice requires accompaniment for an exam, try to arrange this well in advance and have more than one practice session. There are too many other things for students to think about in an exam without having to worry about whether they've counted their bars rest correctly as well.

○ **Backing tracks:** Make using of backing tracks/CDs so students can practise with the accompaniments before they meet with an accompanist. Import the tracks into Speedshifter (see Idea 39) so students can practise at different speeds.

Top tip

Always try to teach other repertoire around a similar standard before embarking on the exam syllabus. Working at exam pieces for more than a term can result in them becoming stale and uninteresting.

Taking it further...

There are many different examination boards: ABRSM; Trinity; London College of Music; Rock School to name but a few. All teachers and students should agree which exam board best suits their needs – each examination board has variations in the syllabus requirements.

"I created my prompt sheet and that helped me work out all the answers."

Any exam board's Grade 5 theory examination can be challenging. This idea provides the guidelines for a prompt sheet that the student can memorise and then create in the examination. It is a useful tool for achieving success!

Teach your students how to write out this prompt sheet from memory at the start of their exam. It will take about 5–10 minutes, but theory exams do have generous timings, especially at Grade 5.

○ **Keyboard:** Draw a picture of a keyboard.

○ **Circle of fifths:** Draw the circle of fifths with the order of sharps and flats along with major and relative minors.

○ **Scale patterns:** Write down the order of tones and semitones in the major scale and melodic and harmonic minors.

○ **Example scales:** Write down example scales to reference for the order of tones and semitones – use C major and A melodic harmonic minors.

○ **Intervals:** Using the scale of C major, write down all the intervals on a stave, making a note of how many semitones, e.g. C–D flat (minor 2nd – one semitone); C–D (major 2nd – two semitones), etc.

○ **Grand stave:** Write down the notes of the treble clef from middle C upwards and of the bass clef from middle C downwards.

○ **Order of sharps and flats:** Write out the key signatures of 6 sharps (F sharp major) and 6 flats (G flat major) to ensure the correct positioning of accidentals.

○ **Clefs:** Write out each of the clefs showing the position of middle C next to each.

Top tip

Suggest your student uses a highlighter pen in the examination to highlight key words in the questions.

Bonus idea !

If your student is doing past theory papers, encourage them to write out a theory prompt sheet each time. This will help them to consolidate the information and get quicker at reproducing it.

80 Musical knowledge tests

"I'm never sure what they are going to ask, how to prepare my student or what template to provide for a brief programme note."

Many examinations now offer an alternative test of musical knowledge from the earliest levels and some higher level (e.g. Diploma) exams have a mandatory viva. This idea provides a quick summary of the kind of questions your students may be asked.

Musical knowledge tests

Firstly, check the exact requirements of the examination in terms of what can be asked within the viva or musical knowledge test and prepare your student specifically. Questions can be asked in different ways, so make sure your student can answer them in all contexts, e.g. they may know that the note is a semi-quaver, but if they were asked how many semi-quavers there are in a crotchet, could they answer?

Here is a quick checklist of questions commonly asked in a musical knowledge element of an examination including the higher grades, or viva.

○ **Title:** What is the significance of the piece's title and how does it relate to the music?

○ **Elements of the score:** Can all elements of the written score be explained – key signature, time signature, note letter names, identifying rests and time values by number and name, dynamics, Italian terms, repeat marks, ornaments, etc?

○ **Intervals and harmony:** Can intervals be identified in the music and, at more advanced stages, modulations and cadences, relative minors, tonic triads of keys and related keys used in the music?

○ **Rhythmic devices:** Can rhythmic devices like syncopation or augmentation be explained?

○ **Scale patterns:** Can scales, modes and arpeggio patterns in the music be recognised?

○ **Structure:** Can the structure be identified, e.g. AB (binary) ABA (ternary) ABACA (rondo)?

○ **Likes and dislikes:** Can the student explain why they 'like' or 'dislike' a piece of music?

○ **Practice strategies:** Can a student give practice strategies for learning tricky parts of the music?

○ **Instrument knowledge:** Can the student explain how their instrument works and what good posture is?

○ **Style and period:** What is the style and period of the music?

○ **Composer and context:** Does the student know about the composer and the context to the music written, e.g. is it part of a greater work?

81 GCSE and A-level performances

"Sir says I have to play a piece for my GCSE — it is next week!"

If you have students who are taking GCSE music, you will no doubt at some point be required to help them find and prepare a suitable performance piece. This idea gives a few pointers to help!

Take the time to find out about the assessment criteria of the examination board being used, and help your students prepare with plenty of time. Think about the following:

Top tip

However good your student is, it doesn't pay to play pieces of a higher level than that required. If GCSE requires a Grade 5 piece, playing a Grade 7 piece only puts the 'perfection' level at risk.

Taking it further...

In nearly every examination syllabus you can find a piece of the appropriate grade that is easier to play than some others. They are the ones to choose!

Bonus idea

Check timings as penalties can result from a piece being too long/short.

● **Accompanist:** If the student is performing a solo piece that requires an accompaniment, consider employing a professional accompanist. If one school only has a few performers, consider making up a group of local schools who can all use the same pianist.

● **Repertoire:** Choice of repertoire is very important. Opt for 'easier' rather than something that stretches the player to the extent that they may not feel totally confident, but make sure it covers all the requirements in the syllabus.

● **Ensemble performances:** Consider an ensemble performance rather than solo – it can often include a member of staff playing, which can add quality of tone and precision to the playing. Working in ensembles is also one of the best and nicest ways for students to develop negotiation skills and also encourages ownership of their performance.

● **Accuracy:** Accuracy matters: every little articulation and dynamic needs to be accurately observed.

● **Dress rehearsal:** For A-level students in particular it pays to have a good dress rehearsal well in advance – giving time to make adjustments if necessary. Many schools have a concert evening for A-level recitals, which can greatly enhance the sense of occasion and performance.

Teaching to their strengths

"The beautiful thing about learning is that no-one can take it away from you." B.B. King

Developing a 'sixth sense' about how each individual student learns is one of the best tools a teacher can have when helping their student progress.

Every student needs to be taught in a way that they can easily assimilate. All students will find different things harder/easier, so play to those strengths and develop from that point.

Try to identify the approach your student finds easiest, e.g. take a simple two bar phrase and:

- play it to them and ask them to play back

- show them the music and ask them to play it

- give the note names and clap the rhythm and ask them to repeat

- ask them to move the notes on a floor music stave (see Idea 43) and then play them.

Once you have developed your sixth sense about how your student learns, think of ways to play to those strengths, e.g.

- Some learners are quite 'academic' and enjoy exploring the nitty-gritty of music. When learning a new piece, explore with them the key, structure and form, and ask them to research about the composer for the next lesson.

- Some students respond well to practical approaches to learning – explore some of the practical ideas in this book, e.g. Ideas 28 and 51)

- Explore Stephen Malinowski's Music animation machine on YouTube (see Idea 33). These are fantastic animated scores that really help some students to understand music in a very visual way.

Top tip

Think about ways to help students with aspects they may find more difficult, e.g. a student who finds playing by ear easy, may struggle with sight-reading. Take a longer-term view to developing note-reading skills (see Ideas 28 and 40).

Taking it further...

Pairing together two students who learn best in different ways can be beneficial to both.

83 Rome wasn't built in a day

"Approach learning an instrument slowly and steadily, like the tortoise in 'The hare and the tortoise'."

Music learning is a life-long pursuit and progress can be achieved sometimes very slowly. If a student is struggling, success can be achieved through breaking the learning process into very small steps.

There are times when our students just can't move on. At this point, the following questions and activities can be helpful. We should also recognise that the most important thing is that the student is enjoying music. Avoid doing things that can be damaging to their development of a life-long love of music.

○ Realistic expectations: What are they able to achieve comfortably?

○ Checking understanding: Check the student can articulate back to you exactly what you expect them to achieve. Can they give you details of how they will tackle a difficult passage notationally or technically?

○ Break tasks down: Look at ways with your student to break a task down. Be careful to not just 'tell' them how to do it. They may come up with some more interesting strategies you haven't thought of, and if it is their suggestion, they will also take some personal ownership of it.

○ Different approaches: Try lots of different ways to teach the same thing using a range of seeing, hearing and doing activities (see Idea 69).

○ Self-belief: Try to instil a sense of belief in your student that they can succeed. Comment on all the positives and avoid criticism. Avoid the 'mistake police' (see Idea 7).

Top tip

Record your student and then replay this recording six months later so they can hear the progress they have made over a longer period of time.

Managing the 84
transfer student

"I really appreciated getting a report from their previous teacher — it made the transfer so easy!"

Taking on a new student from another teacher presents a number of challenges, the main one being that we can never be fully aware of what has been covered and what has not in the student's music education. Evaluating 'where a student is' takes time.

The best approach is to try to find out as much as you can:

○ **Ask the previous teacher:** It's best to try to get as much information about the student's previous lessons before you begin teaching. If possible, try to have a conversation with the previous teacher to be given insight on what material and approach has been used. This may not be possible or appropriate -– especially if a student has given up and is now returning to lessons. However, where appropriate, do try.

○ **Ask the parents:** Get as much information from the parents/carers about what has gone on before, if you are able to, especially if the student has given up previously and is returning to the instrument. Communicate to them what your teaching style and philosophy is.

○ **Talk to the student:** Simply ask the student what they have done before and encourage them to bring all their previous books, exam mark sheets, or whatever material they have. Build up as much of a picture as possible.

○ **Be gentle:** Remember, a new student will be trying to adjust to your teaching style and it can be a steep learning curve. Don't make their learning curve too steep and give lots of reassurance and praise. Keep channels of communication open (see Idea 5).

Top tip

Provide a report for any student you are transferring to a new teacher. This will be valuable for the teacher and also your student.

85 Independent learning

"We must strive to make ourselves redundant for our pupils."

Independent learning is a valuable skill for any student. To be independent, a range of skills need to be nurtured within a student, including developing good practice habits, excellent reading skills, sound technique, resilience to not give up when things get difficult, finding appropriate support and problem-solving skills.

Here are some ideas for how to encourage these important independent skills:

○ **Good practice habits:** This includes how to break down a piece into manageable steps, spotting repeats and patterns, not working from beginning to end, etc. (see Idea 52).

Top tip

Give students a range of independent learning tasks to complete over time, e.g. learning a self-chosen piece of music without support, researching about a composer for background information, arranging a performance opportunity at school without support.

Taking it further...

Encourage your students to attend live performances. Being inspired by others provides good role models and can encourage students to keep learning.

○ **Excellent reading skills:** Although not possible for everyone, this is a huge benefit to musical independence. Provide lots of practice in and out of lessons (See Idea 60).

○ **Sound technique:** Address problems immediately, model good posture and use useful studies (see Ideas 30–31).

○ **Resilience:** Create a culture of 'taking responsibility' by asking a student if they should have approached things differently.

○ **Finding appropriate support:** Encourage your student to find support (not just from yourself), e.g. from friends and relatives and online forums (used safely).

○ **Problem-solving:** Don't give your students all the answers on a plate. Encourage them to solve problems independently, such as developing different ways to practise a challenging passage or learning about a style of music to improve interpretation.

○ **Recording themselves:** This will help them to self-assess. If they are taking exams, you could provide the student with the exam criteria to help with this (available in most syllabuses or online).

Specialist teaching

"I had to ask myself, did I have what they needed to get through an audition for a music conservatoire?"

With a very talented student or even a student with specific needs like a learning difficulty, if we feel the student isn't reaching their potential there are times when we need to pass them on to another teacher or a music school such as a junior conservatoire or specialist music school.

How do you know when to pass your student on?

○ You can't demonstrate the music they are learning effectively.

○ They make such rapid progress and appear to be very gifted, but in the time of the lesson you can't cover all aspects of music-making, including composing, improvising, playing by ear and theory. They need a specialist conservatoire where everything is offered.

○ You don't feel you are inspiring them like you did earlier.

○ You don't have the knowledge to teach the advanced technique they need to tackle difficult repertoire.

○ You don't think your teaching is helping them achieve their potential.

Where do you send them?

Contact your local music hub or Music Mark (**musicmark.org.uk**) to find out about teachers with experience of teaching the gifted and talented or SEND. For very gifted students, you might consider:

○ **Junior conservatoires/Centres for Advanced Training:** Junior conservatoires (such as Junior Royal Northern College of Music, Manchester) or Centres for Advanced Training – CATS (such as Yorkshire Young Musicians) tend to meet at weekends during term-time. A full list is available in the British Music Education Yearbook. Auditions are usually held in the Spring term.

○ **Specialist music schools:** For example, Chethams (Manchester), The Purcell School (London), Yehudi Menuhin School (Surrey), St Mary's Music School (Edinburgh), Wells Cathedral School (Wells, Somerset).

Top tip

If your student has special educational needs like dyslexia or autism, perhaps they may need a teacher trained to work with these students? Alternatively, see if you can get further training yourself to work more effectively with the student (see Ideas 14–16).

87 Teacher roles

"My teacher's great, even if she can be a bit scary! But she's the first person I go to if I've got a problem."

A good teacher's role is to support their students in as many ways as they can. To do this requires building a strong professional relationship with your students and showing commitment to them, but also to be committed to developing yourself and not neglecting your own Continuing Professional Development (CPD).

Commitment to your students

◦ Expectations: Just as you will expect students to understand your expectations of them (see Idea 89), make sure they understand what to expect from you.

◦ Build a professional relationship with your students: Develop a professional relationship with your students where respect is equal on both sides and you can enjoy making and experimenting with all sorts of music.

◦ Being flexible: Although there are various curriculums that we can possibly follow, no two students will ever be the same. Being flexible and thinking about different routes for different pupils is essential (see Ideas 8–18).

◦ Being understanding: Tune in to the realities of today's students' lives: pressure from schools, exams, parents, etc. can all result in periods when your students' attention and time given to music practice may be seriously reduced. Have some more relaxed activities available for these lessons rather than 'sticking to the plan' at all costs, e.g. duets (sight-reading), improvisation (simple harmony exercises), Dalcroze work (see Ideas 60–61), practical musicianship skills, singing, etc.

Top tip

Wanting to be liked can be a dangerous thought for young teachers. Gaining respect comes from being good at your job, not being over-pally with your students (see Safeguarding, Idea 99)

Build a professional relationship with parents/carers: Talk to parents and carers (see Idea 88) and build a mutually-supportive relationship with them. Agree how best they can assist. Some parents/carers may offer practical help, e.g. serving tea and biscuits or printing out programmes for a concert you might put on for your students.

Continuing Professional Development (CPD)

A teacher is often seen as the fount of all knowledge yet, particularly in the early days of teaching, there is a huge amount that we can't possibly have learnt and understood.

One of the teacher's greatest skills to learn is acceptance of your shortcomings alongside confidence in your ability to solve queries and problems because you have learnt where and how to find answers.

Remember that we will never know everything so we should never stop learning:

- Look for CPD courses.
- Go and listen to masterclasses.
- Arrange to sit in on other teachers' lessons.
- Go on a 'summer school'.
- Find a private mentor (see Idea 91).

Taking it further...

Here are some ideas of where to look for CPD:
- Local music hub
- ABRSM training events
- Teacher forums
- Professional bodies, such as Musician's Union (see Idea 98)
- Music Mark and the Music Education EXPO run by Rhinegold.

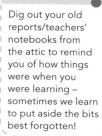

Bonus idea

Dig out your old reports/teachers' notebooks from the attic to remind you of how things were when you were learning – sometimes we learn to put aside the bits best forgotten!

88 The role of parents/carers

"I really want my parents to come to my school concerts!"

Parents and carers have a difficult role to play in supporting everything about their child's life. Every child is different – and so are the parents! However, it is important for parents and carers to understand that students make greater progress when they feel supported in their music. They may not know how best to do this, so here are some pointers to share with them to help.

Home practice

To help encourage students to practise at home, encourage parents/carers to:

○ **Establish a routine:** An expected time (preferably more than one) and length of practice (never too long, but preferably every day) helps establish the importance of a practice routine so that it can become a habit.

○ **Take a step back:** Allow their child the space to develop ideas themselves (standing over a student rarely achieves good results) and focus only on how things have improved that day.

○ **Observe practice:** Often the best place for parents/carers to observe practice is from the next room or the kitchen so that they can hear what is going on, be appreciative of audible improvements and offer support if some bits are causing problems, but are not standing over their child.

○ **Leave 'teaching' to the teacher:** Parents and carers should be wary of offering technical advice – otherwise they may inadvertently contradict what the teacher has said or cause confusion.

Anecdote 💬

Several parents have told me how they have managed to encourage their children to do regular practice by introducing a regular morning slot before school, even though it means getting up very early! The children are fresh and there are *usually* no other distractions. Once the routine is established, it apparently just becomes a normal part of family life.

Incentives: Parents/carers might want to be prepared to provide incentives to help when there are difficult things to learn, e.g. very small chocolates lined up on the music stand (only allowed for 'success') have been known to solve the problem of learning tricky scales.

Performance confidence

To help develop performance confidence, encourage parents/carers to:

- accept upcoming performances as opportunities to be explored and enjoyed rather than a pass or fail situation

- praise rather than criticise – leave any criticism to the teachers who will have a fuller understanding of how the performance fared within the current progress and playing levels

- avoid making comparisons with other students, just appreciate every performance for its merits.

Attending concerts/performances

- Encourage parents/carers to try to attend all of their child's performances.

- Provide parents/carers with details of local concerts that you think their children will find inspiring. Many will enjoy taking their children and having some quality time with them.

Top tip

It is relatively easy to print a little reminder card to give to parents when lessons commence containing suggestions for how they might help (and might not help!) their child progress.

89 Committed students

"Every student is an individual; I try to have a bespoke approach for each of them."

Developing a student's enthusiasm and willingness to learn requires thinking about the student outside the lesson itself. Here are some ideas to help your quest for happy, committed learners.

Student notebook

All students should have their own notebook. This may be something you write in, but it can also be really useful if students write in it too, e.g.

○ Ask them to write their own notes on the lesson and what to practise – this can show whether or not they are really grasping the ideas offered.

○ Encourage them to write (in agreement with the teacher) their short- and long-term goals. Include, if appropriate, performances such as music festivals, school performances, examinations, etc. Accept that some students want to learn 'for pleasure' and be able to play for themselves.

Commitment

Discuss your expectations with your students (see also Idea 87), e.g.

○ To attend lessons punctually and regularly.

○ To be prepared for lessons and bring all necessary equipment (instrument, music, etc.) to every lesson.

○ To observe a regular practice schedule between lessons.

○ To be open and honest about their learning. (They need to know you will listen if they have concerns.)

Taking it further...

You might additionally like to consider (when your students' standard is getting more advanced), that they help some younger students, under the guidance of a teacher.

Once your students have demonstrated their commitment, encourage some additional pointers with them for their development, e.g.

○ A willingness to broaden their musical understanding through researching and listening. (The internet provides amazing access to a huge array of music, e.g. Spotify; imslp.org; GarageBand; YouTube, etc.)

○ A willingness to join extra-curricular groups, e.g. chamber music ensembles, bands, orchestras, choirs, etc.

The work–life balance checklist

"I realised I needed some more 'me time' in my week."

Many instrumental and singing teachers work in a variety of settings, often in a self-employed capacity, making the work–life balance difficult to achieve. This idea gives a few thoughts to consider when trying to get this balance right.

Define for yourself what a good work–life balance is for you. The following considerations may be useful, but remember, it is different for everyone.

❯ Have some 'me time': Do something for yourself – just for the sake of enjoyment.

❯ Have some family time: What family time would be good in your house? For example, this might be playing games with your children, storytime, going to visit your mum…

❯ Have a night out: When was the last time you went out with your partner or a friend?

❯ Exercise is important: Do you do any exercise? Could you fit some in?

❯ Relaxation time: What do you find most relaxing to do (reading, playing music, doing sport)? Could you do more of this each week?

❯ Sleep: Are you getting a good night's sleep on a regular basis?

❯ Switch off from work: Do you constantly think about work when you are not working? How can you distract yourself?

Top tip

List all the activities you do in the day. Have a look at the proportion of time you give to work compared to other activities.

Bonus idea

Know when to switch off PCs and phones and do something totally unrelated to work. Time away from work can help you think more creatively and with better perspective.

91 Mentors and mentoring

"My mentors have enriched my playing, my teaching, my musicianship and my life!"

Having your own mentor is a bit like a personal trainer, but generally far nicer and less painful in outcome. Likewise, accepting a colleague in to view your teaching and discuss it with you can be an initially daunting but ultimately fulfilling experience.

Feedback from colleagues

There are many ways to consider aspects of your teaching in relation to your effectiveness as a teacher. Perhaps one of the most useful is to ask a colleague to give you feedback on your work. Here are some thoughts on how to develop this working relationship.

❍ Arranging for colleagues to give feedback: With a small group of colleagues arrange to view each other's lessons and give feedback.

❍ Positive and constructive feedback: When giving feedback remember to be positive and constructive. Criticism, however well meant, can be destructive.

❍ The positive sandwich: When giving feedback, use the positive sandwich approach: say something positive; give pointers for development; say something positive, e.g. *'You started really well; perhaps you could give a little more focus to the ideas you were trying to put across so suggestions are more punchy; you obviously have a good relationship with your student."*

Working with a mentor

A mentor can be a 'critical friend' – they are there for your benefit and will be able to discuss things openly in a way a colleague may not feel able to do.

Top tip

As a first step, you may like to video your own teaching (obtain parental permission from the students' parents first) in order to make a first assessment of yourself. Remember that your voice will never sound the way you think it would, so don't be put off – look beyond the embarrassment!

● **Choosing a mentor:** When looking for a mentor, choose someone who has a similar ethos about teaching and performing. The biggest name isn't necessarily the person to whom you can relate most easily.

● **Building a relationship with your mentor:** Build a relationship with a mentor you trust so that you can arrange to bounce new ideas off them before you drop your students in it.

● **Mentor observations:** Allow your mentor to view your teaching over time so they can get a good overall picture of how you work – being an instrumental/singing teacher encompasses a lot more than can be observed in a single lesson.

Student feedback

With your more senior students, you could ask them to review the lesson at the end.

● Did they come to the same conclusions as you (very rare!) and if not, why did they pick up on the things of which you were unaware?

Becoming a mentor

Think of becoming a mentor yourself – perhaps with like-minded colleagues, but also with maturing, more advanced young musicians: we all tend to teach how we ourselves were taught, so helping them on to the first rung of the teaching ladder in their late teens will give them confidence to do more teaching in the future.

If you find this a particularly enjoyable task, look at developing more by, perhaps, working with a Continuing Professional Development (CPD) team backed by a professional body.

Taking it further...

Arrange a mentor tea party (or curry night) to have a good get-together and discussion about teaching and what you are all learning by venturing into the mentoring arena.

92 Create a teacher support group

"They understand my problems and provide wise advice!"

Teaching is a process in which we continually interact with others. Our own personal well-being and happiness can directly affect our ability to successfully educate our students. Creating a support group with like-minded colleagues can provide the support we need to be our best.

Who?

Do you have colleagues that you particularly get on with? A small group of teachers who know each other already may really appreciate getting together for a coffee (or other social gathering) and to discuss problems and solutions for their teaching.

Taking it further...

Check out Nic Marks's talk about happiness and well-being: *The Happy Planet Index.*

Anecdote

Over the years I have set up a number of informal teacher support groups. I have gained many ideas, discovered lots of new repertoire, and found solutions to a whole range of problems linked with my students and the job in general. They have always been lovely social occasions and provided a sense of community.

Why?

A sense of community can really help us not to feel lonely in our profession. Remember that 'a problem shared can feel like a problem halved'! Instrumental and singing teaching can be quite stressful, so talking to like-minded colleagues can be helpful in many ways, including supporting your own well-being.

Where?

You can simply meet at each other's houses, or at local coffee shops. The venue could be suggested or hosted by each member of the group in turn.

What?

The group can decide different topics in advance, e.g. reviewing pieces in a new exam syllabus; discussing ways to deal with a student or parent that someone is having difficulties with; sorting out technical problems, etc. There are lots of possibilities!

When?

People are busy so perhaps meeting every term or half-term may be the most realistic.

"It is so lovely to be able to sing in a group but not be in charge!"

As teachers we can do so much teaching that we can neglect our own playing and singing. It is important to make sure that we see our own learning as a continual journey.

Play your instrument for enjoyment

It is lovely to just play what you love, without any other goal apart from enjoyment.

Practise with kindness

When practising yourself, remember the positive ways you encourage your students to practise (it can be too easy to be more crictical on ourselves!)

Ask yourself:

❍ How can I focus on what I have achieved and not on what I haven't?

❍ What am I finding difficult in the music I am studying? What is possible?

❍ What are the different ways to practise?

Strategies for progress

❍ Try breaking practice tasks into much smaller achievable chunks.

❍ Find easier repertoire by the same composer, which is similar in style.

❍ Find studies or exercises that develop the technique needed for the music being studied.

Find inspiration

Attend live concerts, attend local festivals, talk to colleagues, find inspiring blogs and remind yourself what you love about music, attend masterclasses.

Taking it further...

Consider doing a performance diploma (ABRSM, Trinity and London College of Music all provide them). You could have some lessons. The ISM and **Musicteachers. co.uk** have lists of teachers.

Bonus idea

Set yourself goals. Actively seek out performing opportunities, e.g. join a local orchestra, choir or other ensemble, arrange to play duets with a colleague? Perform at your student concert or enter a music festival – some festivals do have classes for adults (visit the British Federation of Music Festivals website: **federationof festivals.org.uk**)

94 Marketing your business

"How can I let people know about me?"

Marketing your business can be achieved through online sources, word of mouth, posters and leaflets, etc. People expect to be given detailed information on the services they are receiving.

When producing promotional information about yourself and setting up your business, think about:

Top tip

A good website to use to market yourself is **MusicTeachers.co.uk**.

Taking it further...

How are you going to promote yourself?
- Word of mouth
- Posters
- Cards at the local supermarket or post office
- Business cards
- A basic website
- Using social media, e.g. Facebook and Twitter.

Bonus idea

Recommendation by word of mouth is highly valuable, especially when teaching children. Parents of current students can do the marketing for you.

What are your key selling points?

- Are you good with young children or adults? Are you able to teach more advanced students or students with SEND?

- Do you teach a wide range of music from pop to jazz/classical?

- Do you enter students for exams?

- Are you good at motivating children?

- What are your qualifications?

How much will you charge?

- Price your services competitively (but not cheaply, which may imply poor quality). (See Idea 96.)

- Are you going to be a mobile teacher? If so, remember to charge for your fuel and set a fee that takes into account travelling time.

Where are you going to teach?

- Is the room comfortable (not cold) and are the instruments good quality (if the students are using them)?

- Is there a waiting area, toilet and adequate parking? Are the neighbours happy about it?

- Have you checked out home and car insurance if you plan to use either for your business?

- Have you thought about Health and safety and done a risk assessment? (See Idea 100.)

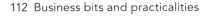

Working in schools – good practice

"Flexibility and teamwork by any practitioner in my school is something I value highly."

As a visitor to a school you need to ensure you fit in with normal school practices. Professional boundaries, good communication and flexibility are always a good start!

Here are some pointers for good practice:

○ Recognise that you are a guest in the school: If you feel that your student has a special educational need or highly sensitive safeguarding issues, always report these to the school SENCO or designated safeguarding officer. Do not contact parents directly or discuss it with the child.

○ Reporting methods: Try to ensure your attainment reporting methods complement the school's. It can be useful to provide the school with a copy (although check this with the parent/carer if you are self-employed). This can highlight useful information to the school they may not be aware of.

○ Behaviour and reward policies: It is good to be aware of these (policies can be requested from the school). A student may do something praiseworthy in their instrumental lesson that can be rewarded by the school. Students should also have to follow the same standards of behaviour in instrumental lessons as they do in class. Some schools will present exam certificates in assemblies.

○ Be flexible and solutions-focused: It is important to be understanding with schools (as far as possible). If there are problems with room availability or difficulty releasing students from class, try to work with the school to come up with a positive solution.

Top tip

Schools are very busy places. The student's needs come first, which means that some communication about school dates or timetables may not be communicated to you. Try to be independent by checking the school website for dates like training days, school trips, exams and sports events.

Bonus idea

Find out who is the SENCO (responsible for students with special educational needs) and the designated safeguarding officer. Have their contact details available ready for any sensitive situations.

96 Contracts and payment

"Get things in writing to protect you and the people you work with."

It's a good idea to set up your teaching as a professional business with contracts and invoices. Everyone needs to be clear on what is expected of them.

Here are some considerations:

○ **Business bank account:** Set up a business bank account and, if possible, get your students' parents to set up standing orders with their bank to pay you. They can do this online or by filling in a form.

○ **Terms and conditions:** Provide a contract outlining your terms and conditions.

○ **Missed lessons:** Make it clear what your policy is on missed lessons. Some teachers ask for 24 hours notice for illness but make up the lesson; others fully charge for all lessons; others only charge for what they teach. It's up to you.

Top tip

Join a professional organisation like the Musicians Union (MU) or Incorporated Society of Musicians (ISM). These organisations provide template contracts for you to use for both teaching in schools and privately.

Bonus idea

A termly newsletter can be helpful for parents outlining details of dates for the term, including any concerts and exam sessions.

○ **Leaving policy:** Again, it is personal choice for what notice period you require for leaving.

○ **Payment policy:** Are you going to ask for payment weekly, a month in advance, half termly or termly?

○ **Cancellation policy:** Ensure that you communicate well in advance your own availability and details of lessons you won't be teaching.

○ **Invoicing:** Provide a clear invoice with your contact details, price of the lessons, dates covered and date payment is due.

○ **Lesson rate:** Decide how much to charge, based on your experience and training along with the rates charged by other teachers in the area. The MU and ISM have details of recommended rates, too.

○ **Payment records:** Keep good records of payments and have contact details so you can get in touch with people by e-mail or phone if there are any problems.

"What do I need to do about tax returns?"

If you are self-employed, you will need to fill in a tax return each year and keep required up-to-date records. This idea is intended to help you get started and provide helpful hints.

If you are likely to earn any money that is not taxed under PAYE you will need to file your own tax return. You will first of all need to register with HMRC as self-employed (hmrc.gov.uk).

Do I need an accountant?

The HMRC website is becoming more and more user-friendly and so, if you are feeling confident, there is nothing to stop you filing your own online returns. Alternatively, find an accountant – but obviously, they will charge you for the service.

Keeping records

The HMRC website has clear guidelines. Here are a few pointers to get you started:

○ Keep a cashbook or use a spreadsheet: Record earnings on one side and your business expenses on the other. Keep your receipts and any other useful pieces of information, number them sequentially and file them. Record the reference numbers in your cashbook.

○ What can you claim for? You can claim for expenses that are wholly and exclusively for your business. (See 'expenses if you are self-employed' on the HMRC website for more information).

○ Keep a record of all income: Remember that *all* your income should be included, whether it is paid by cheque, online or in cash.

○ Put aside money for tax: If you are likely to pay tax on your net income because it exceeds the amount of your Personal Allowance, ensure that you have put money aside to pay the tax bill.

○ Supporting documents: You do not have to submit supporting documents (e.g. P60s, receipts, etc.) to HMRC but you must retain them for not less than six years as they can ask for evidence.

> **Top tip**
>
> It really pays to keep on top of things – try and institute a weekly routine when things are fresh in your memory and you still have the receipts.

98 Professional bodies

"Do I have to feel so alone as a music teacher?"

There are many different groups of musicians who have formed a 'support group' which has, over the years, grown and expanded to national and sometimes international levels. Joining a professional body can put you in touch with like-minded professionals so that you can benefit from each others' experiences.

Joining one of these professional bodies is, in most cases, straightforward – they are happy to receive your annual subscription! In some cases you may be required to produce a reference or recommendation from a serving member.

Top tip

Here is a list of some of the more obvious associations to investigate, but an internet search for professional music bodies will give many more: Musicians' Union; Incorporated Society of Musicians; European String Teachers Association; European Piano Teachers Association; European Guitar Teachers Association; British Flute Society, etc.

Taking it further...

If there isn't an association in your area, why not start one yourself?

Here are some top reasons why you might like to join a professional organisation:

○ Magazine: Most have a regular magazine or journal which is informative and helpful for your own development

○ Summer schools and CPD sessions: Many run summer schools or professional development sessions for their members and non-members.

○ Meeting like-minded colleagues: There will be opportunities for meeting with like-minded colleagues who are sharing an aim to develop their teaching skills.

○ Insurance cover: Some organisations may include automatic insurance cover for some of your instruments/music activities and public liability insurance – but ensure you check the small print.

○ Help and advice: Some organisations can give you help and assistance, e.g. checking contracts; questioning changes in work situations, etc.

○ Local meetings: There may be regular meetings in your locality covering a variety of teaching topics where you will be able to share experiences and perhaps gain ideas for your own teaching.

"The safety of students in our care is all our responsibility."

All teachers need to be aware of the current safeguarding legislation. Those who work for a music hub or school should be given training. Those working on their own will benefit from attending a safeguarding course.

Looking after our students is just as important as looking after ourselves. We all need to be shown appropriate care and consideration.

◦ Safe teaching space: Ensure your teaching space is a safe space, especially if you are using any electrical equipment or large/heavy instruments.

◦ One-to-one lessons: Instrumental teaching can be the one situation in a child's education where they receive one-to-one attention. Therefore, all instrumental and singing teachers should be aware that they are in a privileged position and may be more likely to be entrusted with personal information. Make sure that the correct safeguarding procedures are followed.

◦ Your actions: Ensure that all your actions as a teacher cannot be misinterpreted. If you have discussed appropriate touching with both parents and students and they are comfortable with it, <u>always</u> ask 'May I show you?' before explaining a technical issue that involves any touching – preferably, have a parent in the room. Remember that some students may not be comfortable with any contact at all, in which case you must abide by their wishes. If in any doubt, **don't touch**.

◦ Safeguarding training: If you are not provided with safeguarding training by an employer, take some time to visit some online training sites. National helplines such as Childline (0800 1111) and NSPCC (0808 800 5000) have staff who are very experienced and helpful.

Top tip

All schools and local authorities have a designated officer responsible for safeguarding who should be contacted if you have concerns about a child or vulnerable adult's safety in any area, including the Prevent strategy. (For more details, visit **www.gov.uk**.)

Taking it further...

Teachers who are employed are required to have an Enhanced Certificate from the Disclosure and Barring Service (DBS). Those who teach privately are unable to ask for a DBS check themselves but may be able to find an organisation (such as the Musicians' Union) that can process an application for them.

100 Health and safety

"Health and safety is mainly 'common sense' and the fundamental principles are straightforward."

Basically, health and safety is about identifying things that could cause harm ('hazards') and then ensuring reasonable measures are in place to prevent such harm occurring. That's it! This is normally achieved by conducting a risk assessment following the steps below.

Three steps for a risk assessment:

Step 1: Identify your activities

Think through your working week and make a list of activities carried out by you or your pupils that are associated with your work (e.g. student walks from their car to your house and sits in the waiting area; setting up a classroom for teaching, etc.)

Top tip

If you are working in school make sure you find out about the school's heath and safety policies. Also, make sure you record any accidents that occur whilst you are working there. They will have a book for you to record these.

Taking it further...

Carrying out these three steps constitutes a basic risk assessment. There are more complicated versions of this process if you want them (see the Health and Safety Executive website: **hse.gov.uk**).

Step 2: Identify the hazards

Think about each of the activities identified in Step 1 in turn and list the hazards (things that could cause harm) whilst conducting the activity. Most hazards fall into one of the following categories which can be used to prompt what to think about:

- Slips, trips and falls
- Manual handling (e.g. lifting heavy objects)
- Electrical
- Noise
- Vehicles
- Falling objects…

Step 3: Safety measures

For each of the hazards identified in Step 2, list measures that can reasonably be applied to prevent harm being caused, e.g. covering all cables for electrical instruments with cable covers to avoid tripping; clearing snow and ice from your drive so pupils don't slip when coming to your lessons.